PRAISE FOR
Mom, There's a Man in the Kitchen and
He's Wearing Your Robe: The Single Mother's Guide
to Dating Well Without Parenting Poorly

"In the voice of a trusted girlfriend, Fisher delivers honest advice, a fresh perspective and comic relief as she guides newly single moms toward the goal of dating well without parenting badly." —*Publishers Weekly*

"This book offers practical advice on balancing dating and parenting, on preparing oneself and one's children for the prospect of dating again and all the possible consequences.... Fisher's clear and humorous approach and down-to-earth advice should help maintain healthy relationships among everyone involved."

—*Library Journal* (starred review)

"This is real-world, on-the-ground stuff.... The blend of dating and parenting is almost seamless in these pages, as in life." —Knight-Ridder News Service

"[Fisher] combines her own wisdom with anecdotal experience from other moms." —*Newsday*

"Warmhearted, wonderful book... Ellie addresses [issues] with heart, humor and savvy.... Ellie's book offers comfort and practical advice from someone who's been there, and made her own inevitable mistakes along the way."

—*Trenton (NJ) Times*

Also by Ellie Slott Fisher

*Mom, There's a Man in the Kitchen
and He's Wearing Your Robe*

DATING
for DADS

The Single Father's
Guide to Dating Well
Without Parenting Poorly

ELLIE SLOTT FISHER
with Paul Halpern, Ph.D.

BANTAM BOOKS

DATING FOR DADS
A Bantam Book / February 2008

Published by Bantam Dell
A Division of Random House, Inc.
New York, New York

Book design by Joseph Rutt

Bantam Books and the rooster colophon
are registered trademarks of Random House, Inc.

Library of Congress Cataloging-in-Publication Data

Fisher, Ellie Slott.
Dating for dads : the single father's guide to dating well
without parenting poorly / Ellie Slott Fisher with Paul
Halpern.
p. cm.
ISBN 978-0-553-38486-4 (trade pbk.)
1. Single fathers—Life skills guides. 2. Dating (Social
customs). 3. Parenting. I. Halpern, Paul. II. Title.

HQ759.915F56 2008
306.874'22—dc22   2007038980

Printed in the United States of America
Published simultaneously in Canada

www.bantamdell.com

BVG   10 9 8 7 6 5 4 3 2 1

For Thelma and Herbert Sayare,
who prove that single parents can date well
without parenting poorly.

Contents

Acknowledgments

At first, I was daunted by the task of finding single dads to interview for this book, because the only ones I knew personally were the ones I had dated. And I wanted to dredge up those old memories as much as a Red Sox fan wants to rehash the 1986 World Series. So, instead, I e-mailed people from various aspects of my life, asking for the names of any single dads who might be interested in being part of this project. I was overwhelmed by the response. I am so grateful, not only to the wonderful dads and the impressive children who let me peek into their lives, but to those people who connected me to them. Thank you for responding to my request: Evie Ferris, Diane Rogers, Lori Frank, Paula Koerte, Sindey Dranoff, Hank Herman, Esther Ganz, Malinda Berardino, Shelley Miller, Susan Cohen, Susie Schultz, Mark Schultz, Susan Whitehead, and Rachel Cantlay.

You led me to a group of men and children who should serve as an inspiration to all single-parent families. Although

I've changed their names in the book, some have given me the honor of thanking them publicly. They include: Adam Waxman, Vince Clews, Ashleigh Clews, Steve Ritzau, David Frelicher, Howard Cove, Max Cove, Jeff Sameroff, Evan Sameroff, Daniel Robinson, David Griffitts, Natalie Griffitts, Marissa Griffitts, Dan Weitzman, Jeff Price, Bill Brauner, Chris Fallon, Kaitlyn Fallon, Scott Sayare, Jack Cantlay, and Melanie Miller.

When a book is completed, every author claims to have had the best editor, but they're wrong. I did. Julie Will not only took a risk on a book for men, but she meticulously and enthusiastically edited these pages. She consistently made me feel as though I was her only author, responding to my queries expeditiously and respectfully. I am grateful to several other people at Bantam Dell, including Nita Taublib, Danielle Perez, Barb Burg, Belina Huey, and Kathleen Baldonado, and to my agent, Susan Cohen, who once again worked tenaciously on my behalf.

A book like this can only be as good as the advice it offers, and for that I turned to a notable group of professionals. A huge thank-you goes to Paul Halpern, who, I knew two minutes into our first interview, was not only an expert on single-parent families, but a kindred spirit as well.

Thank you, too, to my medical experts, Dr. Brad Rogers and Dr. Howard Rosenthal, whose comments should help allay some of the physical concerns men have when they resume dating. And to attorneys Justice Sandra Schultz Newman and Judith E. Siegel-Baum for their brilliant advice on legal issues faced in second marriages and blended families.

Once again, all my friends have been supportive of my work, but a few of them have been needled more than others. So thanks for always asking, and listening: Fran Bank, Helen Bosley, Pam Cohen, Elaine Flatch, Doris Grassi, Mia and Jack Ingham, Elise Katz, Bea Lazaroff, Rebecca Lee, Richard Moore, Fran Rosenbaum, Sally Solis-Cohen, Puddie Sword, Lisa Waldman, and Eileen Wolf. To Jon Roth, who was the second happiest person when my manuscript was completed, thank you for your constant support, editing advice, and love.

No single parent can do it alone without the affection and devotion of her family, which, in my case, includes Thelma and Herb Sayare, the entire Schultz clan, and of course, my two biggest fans: Debra and Noah Fisher. You two make my being a parent a complete and utter joy.

Foreword

by

Paul Halpern, Ph.D.

In my thirty-five years of practice as a clinical psychologist in Philadelphia, I've counseled a large number of single fathers and their children. These men often say they seek therapy not because they are struggling with their divorce or the death of their wife, but out of concern for their kids. I think it is easier for men in our society to enter therapy, at least initially, for the good of the children. It is difficult for men, who are generally reluctant to share their feelings and may see therapy as a sign of weakness, to admit that they need help for themselves. But what all single dads come to realize, eventually, is that they have their own feelings of loss, loneliness, and fear about the future. While these newly single fathers want the best for their kids, they often don't recognize that their own happiness is equally important—especially if they are to rise to the challenge of providing security and emotional nurturance to their children.

Over the years, I have seen many widowed and divorced

men overwhelmed with the thought of dating again. For some, their last date occurred twenty-five years ago, when they worried more about hiding their acne from their date than hiding a woman from their kids. As sophisticated and successful as these men are, when it comes to dating, many of them are substantially less confident. Not only is the world of dating brand-new, but the fact that they are fathers complicates things even further. All of a sudden they are faced not only with the challenge of finding romance again, but with the unexpected burden of increased parental responsibilities.

Finally, a book has been written that reassures these men that they can be terrific fathers without abandoning their own needs. Relationship expert Ellie Slott Fisher understands the unique challenges faced by single parents. As a mother who has been widowed, remarried (briefly), and divorced, all the while raising a son and daughter by herself, Ellie knows firsthand that combining dating with parenting is an imperfect science. She acknowledges that mistakes are easy to make, and that she's made plenty of them herself. But drawing on the lessons she's learned, as well as my insights, and professional information from medical and legal experts, she offers solid, judgment-free advice. Single dads faced with the challenges of having a social life while raising children will find her book immeasurably helpful.

I must admit I wasn't necessarily thinking about the complications of dating as a single father when I received a call from Ellie about this project. I was on vacation in

Maine during the late summer, the time when many therapists close down their offices and get away with their families. She was interviewing therapists who work with
single dads and their children, and one of my former patients had told her about me. Intrigued by the idea of this
book, I met with Ellie to discuss the basic issues of single
fatherhood. Over the next several months, as we delved
into more details, our conversations became deep and rich,
and I realized what a compelling need there was for a
guide like this to help single dads who date.

We also discussed case studies, since my practice includes a significant number of single-father families. I told
her about a recently widowed man who came to see me in
order to help his children deal with the death of their
mother. After some time in family therapy, and once he
felt better about the emotional stability of his children, he
began to face the fact that he, too, was struggling with
feelings of loss and depression. And having never been a
hands-on parent, he was overwhelmed by his new role as
his children's *only* parent. He also realized that after twenty
years of marriage, the thought of dating again terrified
him. Initially, he had a few stumbles. He misread women,
made some bad choices, and vowed more than once to
never date again. But he persevered, and eventually met a
woman with whom he formed a lasting, loving relationship. When it came time to introduce her to his kids—a
difficult process—we dealt with many more issues in family therapy. But today he is very content with his new
wife, and his children have adapted well.

In our conversations, Ellie and I discussed the myriad issues faced by single dads as they begin dating again. Is there a right way to date? Should fathers involve their children in the process? Will the children willingly accept a new woman, a potential stepmother, into their lives? Will it be emotionally damaging for them to see a woman emerge from their father's bedroom? There aren't any easy answers to these questions, but Ellie has constructed a very helpful road map through this rocky terrain.

One thing I've learned after so many years on this side of the therapist's couch is that all single fathers tend to face the same challenges when they begin dating again. Ellie surveyed and interviewed dozens of single dads and children of single fathers for this book. In its pages she shares their stories, which provide a thread of commonality and an emotional resonance with which you will likely relate. If you've ever hesitated before introducing a woman to your kids, or wondered how much affection is too much in front of them, you are not alone. As you read the narratives of the dads profiled here, you may find yourself nodding along in agreement, and feeling understood by someone you've never even met.

Dating for Dads is also filled with examples that offer insight into the thoughts and feelings of your children. You get a behind-the-scenes view into their minds, and Ellie offers therapeutic solutions for your children's problems and techniques for providing them with an emotionally safe environment. You'll find that, regardless of the backgrounds of the dads and children interviewed, all are struggling with the same feelings. It doesn't matter whether you have primary or infrequent custody of your kids, or whether they're young enough to need a babysitter or old enough to be one, your new social life will affect them significantly.

Ellie also unravels the complexities of the women you will date: Are single mothers more sensitive to your children's needs? How do you give a girlfriend attention without neglecting your kids? When, and how, do you meet her kids, if any exist? As a woman who has dated single dads, Ellie gives you the inside scoop on everything you need to know about how to keep her happy without alienating the kids.

I know that *Dating for Dads* will equip you with the tools you need to be a great dad with an active and healthy social life. I believe it will be almost as welcome a bedside companion as the new woman in your life.

Introduction

Did you ever think you'd see a baby-changing station in the men's bathroom of Barnes & Noble? Or a television commercial that depicts a single dad hugging his children after an outing and thanking his ex-wife for allowing him to come along? How about a blockbuster film that portrays a single father who actually raises his kids without the assistance of Mary Poppins?

While other people may find these signs of change surprising or even shocking, as a single dad, you wonder what's taken so long. In the United States alone, one out of every forty-five fathers now heads a family household by himself. That's more than 2.2 million men who spend night after night reminding their kids to brush their teeth and do their homework.

You know the drill. And whether your kids live with you full time, part time, or on occasional weekends and holidays, there's no doubt you love and care for your children as much as any happily married guy—the one who never seems to have to decide between helping his ten-year-old study for a math test and watching the football game with his buddies.

You, on the other hand, get to juggle more balls than the Harlem Globetrotters. You rush home from work so you can coach baseball, and just as you're about to charge out the door with your equipment bag, your hysterical twelve-year-old daughter announces she just got her first period. Later, after you have managed to effectively handle it all and the kids are asleep, you remember (now that the stores are closed) that tomorrow is your day to be snack parent. As you drive to the 7-Eleven, you try to remember what life used to look like, and you wonder where, in all of this, you can possibly squeeze in a social life.

As much as you love your children, there is a void in your life, one aching to be filled with conversation, companionship, and the warmth and affection of an adult of the opposite gender. While the demands of single fatherhood can be overwhelming at times, you shouldn't let them discourage you from dating. It *is* possible to be a great dad and a great lover. Tom Hanks did it in *Sleepless in Seattle*. He got the kid, and he got the girl. So can you.

I know from researching my first book, *Mom, There's a Man in the Kitchen and He's Wearing Your Robe,* how challenging—but rewarding—it can be for single mothers to date while being mindful of their children. What I learned from researching this book is how different this experience is for single dads and how little support exists for men. Ironically, you've always been told it's a "man's world," so not only are you reluctant to seek help, but you think there's something wrong with you if you do. In addition to all your fatherly obligations, you now also must compete for dates with a bunch of ripped twenty-somethings fresh out of law school, do this on Internet dating sites where 60 percent of all visitors online are men looking for women, *and* pull it off even though you haven't been in a healthy sexual relationship in months or even years.

When I walked in the door to conduct my first book talk on single moms and dating, I had anticipated a room full of women. Instead, I was amazed to find, and completely un-prepared for, an audience half filled with men. I had as-sumed that the rules for dating as a single parent were fairly generic and not gender-specific. But as my book talks continued and as single dads kept filling my audiences and participating in the Q&A sessions, I began to understand that when it comes to dating, the issues for single dads and single moms are not the same.

So I set out to interview single fathers and children of single dads—whose names have been changed throughout the book—and discovered that there are differences not only in how you date but also in how your children react to your social life. Sometimes your kids are supportive, even encouraging. Other times they perceive you as a little too wild and irresponsible (you know, a little like them). You have to delicately balance dating with being a respon-sible dad. To accomplish this, it's imperative to understand your own needs as well as those of your kids.

First of all, know that you are not alone. In fact, as I

alluded to earlier, the pool of single fathers is growing rapidly. In the past ten years, the number of households headed by single dads has risen 62 percent, according to the U.S. Census Bureau. And this figure does not take into account the millions of fathers who share custody either part time or occasionally. This increase in single-dad households has come about as more dads are awarded custody, more women relinquish custody for careers, more men seek equal or greater than 50 percent custody to reduce steep child support payments, and many more dads want to be actively involved in their children's lives. In the next seven chapters, I will be sharing the stories of some of these men who, though their circumstances vary, all want to have a meaningful, lasting relationship with a woman while remaining responsible, loving fathers.

When such men choose to date to enrich their lives and consequently their children's (even if it doesn't feel that way at first), the reason they most often cite is a fear of being alone. Unlike women, who immediately surround themselves with friends and family when they become single, men tend to have less of a support network. Clinical psychologist Dr. Paul Halpern, whose wisdom will be shared throughout this book, says men generally find it much more difficult to be unattached. "A lot of people are not ready to date, but the worry of being alone projects them into the dating field sooner," he says. "And men have much greater difficulty with being by themselves. There is a certain level of dependency. Women tend to be more independent and are accustomed to working, raising the kids, and running the household. Most women, even if they have a full-time job, still do 80 percent of the house-work. A lot of men aren't accustomed to this role. One dad called me in tears when all of his underwear turned pink."

If your loneliness is a result of being laundry-challenged, you're probably looking for a housekeeper rather than a mate. And you shouldn't be reading this book, you should be looking in the yellow pages. What you want and deserve unequivocally is a partner—a lover, a friend, a companion. No other relationship can provide you with such security and contentment, as is borne out in several studies on adult happiness. In *The Case for Marriage: Why Married People Are Happier, Healthier, and Better Off Financially,* authors Linda J. Waite and Maggie Gallagher find that not only are married men happier than single men, but their mortality rate is lower. While these statistics certainly make partnership appealing, single parents must approach any new relationship with caution.

One of the reasons for this is that single dads who struggle with being alone sometimes rush into serious relationships, resolutely ignoring red flags the way a Super Bowl quarterback disregards his injury and plays through the pain. Jason is one of these guys. He admits that he dislikes being alone so intensely that he'd rather forgo dinner than eat alone. After his wife died, Jason became involved in a terrible relationship just for the company. "Next year my youngest kid is leaving for college. We're really close, and my life's going to feel so empty when he goes," Jason says. "That's why I hung on to this woman. For me, a bad deal is better than no deal at all."

The information and real-life examples in this book will

help you spot the warning signs of a bad relationship. You'll also receive a few pointers on how to remain rational when your passionate self disconnects from your parenting self. You'll be introduced to Jim, a divorced father of three drawn in by an extremely sexy and good-looking woman he met in a bar. He plowed into a serious relationship, thinking he had found love again. Just when the passion subsided and he was preparing to move on, they found out she was pregnant. Five years later, after the birth of a second child and a miserable second marriage, he is single again, but not before incurring substantial financial and emotional costs for himself—and his kids. Today, he infrequently sees his children from his second marriage, and his older kids no longer trust his judgment.

Jim's not-quite-fatal attraction is somewhat understandable when you consider that most men would have been lured to that woman in the bar. The number one quality men say they are searching for in a woman, not surprisingly, is good looks. In fact, on a list of the ten traits men most often seek in a mate, the first is average physical attractiveness and the second is beauty. Far down the list at number six is intelligence. Women, on the other hand, reverse these attributes when looking for a mate, placing intelligence at number one and physical attractiveness at number six. Being downright handsome lines up at number nine! Hope I just made your day.

Staying mindful of these priorities might help you avoid another pitfall of dating as a single father: mistaking lust for love. Women can do this too, but typically not as often.

Sex is important to them, but so is your job, your relationship with your ex-wife, your financial security, and the car you drive. (No one ever said we weren't shallow just because we place less emphasis on looks!) Men get so unglued and enraptured while in the throes of good sex—especially if it had hibernated during their marriage—that they often think they are falling in love. You may not know it's happening to you, but your kids will. They'll see your glazed-over look, your out-of-character attitude, your sudden attention to grooming, and be repulsed. Just because these kids stay umbilically attached to their video games and stuff their ears with nano-sized cell phones and music devices does not mean they're oblivious to their surroundings. They notice when you take a phone call behind closed doors and when you overdo the Old Spice.

The irony is that kids actually expect Dad to date—more so than Mom. It's caveman versus Madonna (and not the Material Girl). Kids see their fathers as natural hunters and their mothers as nurturers. But this doesn't mean you get off easy, because your children assume that a hunting father can't possibly act intelligently and maturely. After all, you're a guy. You'll fall for the first woman who brings a lasagna to your door upon learning that you're single. And your children will think you've lost your mind. They might even take over your former wife's role and scold you for buying that convertible or whatever extravagance you afforded yourself upon becoming single. (No shame here. We all do it.)

That your kids expect you to date more than their mom

is also a reflection of our social climate. Mothers are nearly universally expected to raise the kids—a conception that fails to give caring fathers the credit they deserve. There is a prevailing assumption that as soon as a man becomes single, he needs a woman to help him manage his life, especially if he has kids. Popular television shows do little to refute this stereotype. Father-bashing sitcoms such as *Everybody Loves Raymond* and *Yes, Dear* paint dads as bumbling incompetents and moms as brilliant saviors. (Although that may change as more shows feature single dads. A study by the Parents Television Council found almost 11 percent more children were being raised by single fathers on prime-time network television during the 2004–5 season than in the previous season.)

Just as kids are slightly more tolerant of Dad's dating, they also have a double standard for their parents regarding sex. Although they cringe at the prospect of their mother having sex, they actually expect you to. Let me clarify that: they expect you to, but they do not want confirmation. You cannot sneak a woman out of the house before your kids wake up and really believe that they won't catch a whiff of her perfume, hear the screen door squeak closed, or find an earring on your bedroom floor. As most of the dads I interviewed discovered, it is a challenge to keep your sex life under wraps with your kids around. And coming to terms with this can be difficult. After all, you are not a teenager anymore. Why should you have to scout out secret places to have sex when you have a perfectly good home for which you pay a substantial mortgage or rent? How unsuave to use your friend's apartment or the backseat of your SUV! But this is what you might resort to in order to keep your children safely removed from your sex life, and you'll be a better father for it.

If you've already started dating again then you know the first question your child asks is not "What does she look like?" or "What does she do?" but "Does she have kids?" Her status as a parent matters to your children. If the answer is yes, your child's thoughts will begin wandering in a hundred directions: *How old are they? Will my dad like them better? Will I have to move into their house? There's no way I'm moving into their house. With my luck, her kids are losers.* While your child projects a dreadful future with this woman, you're not even sure you want a second date.

And yet the possibility that you'll date single mothers this time around is fairly significant. Most single fathers like the idea of dating a woman who's already a mother, thinking she'll naturally be good to their children. You may believe, as one single dad said to me, "Women who have children are less selfish." Translation: they are lower-maintenance. Single moms, on the other hand, are not necessarily looking for parenting help and would be just as happy if you came without kids. The mere fact that you have them is very rarely a deal breaker, but how they impact your relationship with her can be.

In the next several chapters, you'll discover how to navigate this tricky social world where, try as you might to separate your love life from your family life, your relationship with her will be affected by the actions of your children and hers. You will also learn to discern when your child doesn't like her because he's understandably frightened of the changes she'll bring to your family and when it's because he is perceptively on target about her character.

The first rule of dating as a single father is to be truthful with your kids. Honesty may seem like a no-brainer, but single dads often prefer to delay mentioning that they're dating at all until a relationship turns serious. In fact, dads are much less likely than moms to introduce a date to their child. While it's okay to delay the introduction of your child and a woman—which, incidentally, may require the diplomacy of the historic Reagan-Gorbachev meeting—it is not okay to hide from your kids the fact that you're dating. Not only are they entitled to know, but chances are likely they will find out. Either someone else will tell them (and you don't want their mother's spin on it) or you will slip up ("Dad, this isn't my bra!"). When this happens, all those trust credits you've built up will blow away like leaves you so painstakingly raked on a windy day.

There's a delicate balance between honesty and revealing too much. The survey I conducted of more than a hundred fathers and their children indicated that 47 percent of kids want to know that their father is dating, while 17 percent would rather not know. The remaining 36 percent are ambivalent; that means they want to know you are dating but they aren't looking for details.

The ultimate objective of this book is to help you discover that you can be a hunk while also being a dad, and a great one at that. You'll learn how to decode the complicated feminine psyche, why you shouldn't share your Internet date searches with your kids, why you should welcome fix-ups and blind dates, and whether you can set a curfew for your teenager while not having one yourself.

You'll also see that while you may still feel like a teenager, dating is a lot different from what it was when you really were sixteen. Back then you didn't have to shove over car seats or swipe away Burger King crumbs before climbing into the backseat of your car. (This evidence of parenting, by the way, is not a turnoff to women. A caring dad is passionate, adorable, even sexy when he successfully balances being a lover with being a father.) Any relationship you develop now has to have room for your kids. This doesn't mean you acquiesce to them and let them commandeer your social life. It means that you bring to a romantic relationship every part of who you are. It's when you are clearly manipulated by your children—and we all are to some extent—that a woman, mother herself or not, will abruptly stop answering your phone calls.

This book will also help you make decisions regarding marriage, blended families, cohabitation agreements (a kind of prenup without the nuptials), and smart sex. And we'll face any physiological worries, such as impotence and snoring, that may get in the way of achieving the intimacy you crave.

Whether you have primary or joint custody or see your kids on occasional weekends, dating as a dad requires skill, ingenuity, and a liberal dose of patience. Reassure yourself that as a living, breathing man, you are entitled to date, and despite what your snooping neighbor might think about the parade of women arriving at your house every Saturday night (okay, you can dream), you will be a better father for doing so. Dr. Halpern agrees. "Go ahead and date," he advises. "It is reassuring for the kids in the long run. If dads are happy, they will bring more joyfulness to their kids as well." Your children's health and happiness are paramount, but you can't relinquish yours.

I empathize with your situation. I became a single parent when Charlie, my husband of fifteen years, passed away suddenly. Our daughter, Debra, was nine, and our son, Noah, was five. My desire to be a great—no, actually, phenomenal—single parent drove my very existence. I would prove to the world (or at least to my mother-in-law) that I could cook dinner, coach my son's soccer team, keep the laundry under control, and earn a living. I forgot one thing: my life as a sensual, social being. Single moms and dads so diligently strive to provide a secure and normal life for their kids that they often neglect having one themselves, and when they do, the conflicts can be overwhelming.

Under pressure from family and friends to start dating, some fourteen months after being widowed I finally agreed to be fixed up. The dating skills I had acquired twenty years earlier were no longer adequate, especially when it came to keeping my social life apart from my ever-present children. I made mistake after mistake, including allowing my passion to blindly drive me into a serious relationship that ended in marriage and then divorce. (Single women can sometimes confuse lust for love, too!) Balancing the needs of my children, his children, and our relationship as a couple became so complicated that I ignored my better judgment. I wish I'd had single-parent dating advice before I got started. I am now single and dating again, much the wiser.

Before you embark on your new love life, be up-front with your kids and reassure them that no woman will ever take their place in your heart. All children are affected profoundly by divorce or a parent's death. How you perform now as a father—a responsible, self-confident one with his own social life—will set the standard for their future adult relationships. There is no better teacher than you.

1

Breaking News:
Dad Is Dating!

In all likelihood, fifteen or so years ago when you dreamily said "I do," you didn't imagine being single again one day. Yet here you are, unmarried...with children. First you need to refamiliarize yourself with the concept of dating, and then you need to prepare your kids.

How does that well-known adage "See no evil, hear no evil, and speak no evil" apply to the children of a dating dad?

They see everything.

They hear everything.

They speak when the mood strikes them.

Your job as a single father is to raise them, nurture them, support them, and defend them while also reading their minds.

Children often act ambivalent, fooling even the most perceptive father into thinking they just don't care. But one of the consequences of your decision to date again is that their hopes of Mom and Dad reconciling are dashed, which is a tough concept for them to confront head-on. So instead, they conceal their feelings, feigning disinterest if you even hint about going on a date. They are not prepared to witness Dad with another woman, let alone his embarrassing love-struck antics as he falls under the spell of what's-her-name.

The other reason they may hide their true feelings is that they think you'd rather not know what's on their minds. Clinical psychologist Dr. Paul Halpern says children often believe they have no choice but to resign themselves to their father's new social life. "They know that Dad thinks 'toughing it out' is the mature response. You don't whine. You don't complain. Just get over it." Because of this, it can be difficult for your kids to discuss their feelings with you directly. And if you don't broach the subject, neither will they.

Yet while they may be mum about your dating prospects, your family and friends probably have a lot to say. When a death or divorce occurs, those who are closest to you usually are of the opinion (even if they are tiptoeing around the suggestion) that you need a mate. After all, you're a man—you can't possibly raise the kids alone, they think. Though you might have some new tricks to learn—such as telling your kids to sign you up for paper goods rather than cupcakes for the class party—you're sharp enough, loving enough and, ahem, man enough to do just fine. You should date because *you* want to, but take it slowly so that your children have time to process this new development in your life.

Keep in mind, too, that while you are not a mind reader, neither are your kids. You will be considering the possibility of dating again long before they know anything about it, and the news will probably come as a shock to them. If possible, ease them into the idea by talking about it before you actually begin. Let them hear from you, "At some point I'd like to start dating. I'm not sure when that will be, but I don't want you to be surprised." Dr. Halpern warns dads that after a divorce or death of a parent, children need at least six months to a year to process the loss and the change in their family. If one parent is gone they need to solidify their relationship with the remaining parent. After they've had some time to adjust and heal, they will be more open to the possibility that Dad might meet someone new.

Regardless of whether your children's mother remains in their lives, your role as a parent has changed drastically. You've taken on additional responsibilities that may feel foreign if you've always assumed comforting a crying child was Mom's work while disciplining an unruly son was better left to Dad. As a single father, you will do both. You will bring an openness and honesty to your relationship with your children that perhaps didn't exist before. You will do something with your kids you might normally avoid: you will talk about your feelings, and you will listen to theirs.

And that will encourage your kids to do the same.

Parenting Solo: The Widowed Dad

It's difficult for any man to suddenly find himself alone, running a household, and raising the children. Your day-to-day existence is, of course, further complicated by the grief you and your children both suffer. Be patient with yourself and your kids as you go through the stages of loss, including denial, guilt, and anger. It's a long, arduous process. Many of the widowers I interviewed had been accustomed to traditional roles at home—they worked while their wives, even when they held jobs, ran the home and acted as primary caregiver for the kids. When their wives died, they not only lost their mates but also suddenly assumed sole responsibility for everything.

So while you are grieving over the loss of your wife, you're also facing an increased workload. This puts an unfamiliar stress on your whole family. "I found myself very angry for a long time because I didn't like the role I had to play," says Dwight, a fifty-year-old school principal with three daughters. "Before, when my wife was alive, I would help out with the wash but didn't have to do it every day. I wasn't much of a cook. I became a cook. I wasn't into meal planning, but I had to do that. You come home from work and you're tired. I was angry at my deceased wife for leaving me with so much to do. I had to be mad at someone."

Unlike Dwight, who had gradually taken over the household duties during his wife's illness, Conrad had been so entrenched in his time-consuming job as a physician that his wife's unexpected death completely derailed him. Raising his three kids by himself was perplexing, to say the least. Like a lot of fathers who abruptly find themselves in that role, Conrad admitted he wasn't always sure how to handle all aspects of parenting. When his oldest daughter asked permission to pierce the top of her ear, he was nonplussed. "I said, 'I'll ask your mother.' Then I looked up, asked, and replied, 'Your mother says no.' I answer to a higher authority."

Like all men whose marriages end, either because of divorce or death, fifty-four-year-old Conrad feels that he's been unfairly robbed of a future. Everything he and his wife planned together vanished with her premature death. I feel that way, too, sometimes, but self-pity only compounds my loss, punishing me over and over again. I've come to realize that losing a spouse doesn't rob me of a future as much as it creates different experiences and opportunities. In your case, your future may include a new wife, an extended family, or a different home. It's the unpredictability and the hope that lie in the unknown that help you emerge from grief.

Jason dreaded his role as a single father. When his wife, Cynthia, died, he suffered a physical pain so crippling, he says it felt "like someone reached in my chest and ripped out my heart." Deeply in love, they had an equal marriage, sharing all the household chores and financial matters. But when it came to parenting their three sons, Jason had always deferred to Cynthia. "I was afraid of being a parent because my own father had been so mean," he says. "I'd ground the kids for a month. No television for two weeks.

My wife would say, 'Do you know what you're doing to them? You're not even home all day.' "

Emboldened by the task of keeping further disruptions from his children's lives, after the death of their mother Jason tried doing it all: preparing dinner every night, keeping up with the housework, driving the boys to all of their activities, and working full time. The consequences of his Herculean efforts? Two herniated disks, severe stomach discomfort, and a lot of misery and stress. Jason was so focused on his children and work, he never even considered the prospect of a social life for himself.

At first, parenting alone can feel overwhelming and practically impossible. Even Seth, who had been a stay-at-home dad and felt perfectly capable of doing the housework and tending to the kids, was staggered by his new role. When his wife passed away, he assumed the full responsibility of parenting twenty-four hours a day without a break. "I didn't have anyone to bounce ideas off," says Seth. "You don't have your soul mate there to assist you. And then there's the loneliness. All the other losses we handled together. This I had to handle by myself while raising the kids."

Thirty-eight-year-old Gary relates to Seth's situation. His wife, too, had been the principal wage earner. He was twenty when he started a job at a manufacturing company and was introduced to his female boss. Almost instantly, he was smitten. A rich ten-year marriage followed, producing three daughters but ending tragically with his wife's premature death from cancer. At first, friends and neighbors crammed the house, bringing dinners, helping with the girls, and comforting him. But gradually the plates of food and the support stopped coming and Gary, though accustomed to cooking and cleaning, was ill equipped to assume the role of both father and mother. By the time his kids returned to school after the funeral and Gary had resumed work, he was physically and emotionally exhausted.

Like so many widowed dads, Gary allowed himself to *think* about dating and falling in love again, but had no idea when to begin. Dr. Halpern says, "After a loss, a lot of guys say, 'I'm going to put myself into my children, into my work, my tennis game on Sunday. That's enough for me.' That sounds very hollow and empty. If you had something really special, the loss is devastating. I think those are the guys who have the most difficulty finding someone else, because they've had someone great. Some of them need to say, 'My wife was wonderful but not perfect,' which gives them permission to move on."

Timing is a particularly sensitive issue for widowers and the one aspect of their social lives on which everyone offers an opinion. All those family members, friends, and acquaintances who are *not* in your shoes have their own perception of the "appropriate" time for you to get over your loss and begin to date. You won't be able to please everyone on this issue, nor should you try. What you know, and what other people may or may not choose to understand, is that dating again, even falling in love again, never minimizes the love you have for your first wife.

When your second child was born, did you love your first child any less? The decision to begin dating again is yours alone. And while their feelings are always paramount, even your children don't get to make this decision for you.

Precious Time: Divorced Dads

A friend of mine who has been divorced for five years and has partial custody of his children will go out on dates only when his children aren't staying with him. That means every other weekend and half of every week he will not see his current girlfriend. It also means that he goes through girlfriends like professional baseball players go through bats. He says there is no way he'll give up precious time with his kids. Consequently, his social life is sporadic at best.

If you are a divorced dad who has limited custody of your children, you can't imagine taking away from the prized time you have with them to cruise the bar scene. Any decision to begin dating is wrought with emotion and guilt. First you have to get past the hurt and scars left by your divorce, especially if it was less than amicable. Then you have to resolve the guilt about squeezing in a social life when your time with your children is already limited. "I used to be overwhelmed with sadness that I only see them half a month," says forty-four-year-old Robert of his four kids, "but I'm motivated to make the most of the time when I have them." What matters is not how much time you spend with your kids but how you spend that time. Another father, Warren, understands this; living close to his three kids, he makes the most of every moment they have together, even though he sees them less often than when he was married. In his thoughtful words: "You don't measure parenting on the extraordinary days. It's the ordinary days that mark the kind of parent you are."

These ordinary days are the ones that will transform your kids into well-adjusted adults. It never stops being necessary for you to do small loving acts: help them with their homework, commiserate with them when their prom date cancels, grab a bat and a ball and take them to the park. Talk to them—even if it's by phone—about their day. Remain engaged in their daily lives.

Dr. Halpern says, "Reassure them that they will never be rejected or ignored. Even if you meet someone new, your relationship with your kids will not be violated. This stranger will not come between you and them." Your kids may need to hear this from you over and over again—at least as often as you tell them to clean their rooms.

Like widowers, some divorced dads become so stressed by their new single-parenting duties that dating is the farthest thing from their minds. David, a forty-four-year-old engineer, has been responsible for his kids since his wife trimmed down and tightened up and left him for a twenty-two-year-old at the gym. As if being both mother and father weren't challenging enough, David endures a two-hour commute to and from work each day and arrives home after 7:30 P.M. to make dinner for his kids. Like so many of the fathers who have full custody of their children, David thinks a social life for himself will take time away from his responsibilities as the sole parent. It's easy to deny yourself a love life because you feel guilty about the divorce, deluged by your responsibilities as a parent, and worried about your child's feelings. But would you ever discourage your child from having a social life with his peers? As much as he needs to be around other kids to become well-rounded and self-confident, you need to be around adult members of the opposite sex.

Not only do our kids influence our decision to date again, but overtly or tacitly, divorced dads are often hindered by another presence: the ex. If she's not dating, then she quite possibly isn't happy that you are. If she is dating, you may feel extra pressure to get back out there yourself. All of this is compounded by your children universally wishing that Mom and Dad would reconcile. Before telling them you intend to start dating, you must first make sure they understand that your marriage is over. They need to know that while you and their mother love them very much, you and she will never reunite. You may one day meet a woman who will grow to love them, too (because what's not to love?!), but she will never take the place of their mom.

It's All in the Timing

Stan's wife lost a long bout with cancer, and after the funeral his house filled with friends and neighbors bringing precooked dinners, plates of brownies, and baskets of fruit. He politely greeted each one as he leaned against his kitchen counter for support, still in a state of disbelief and exhaustion. His daughter, who had recently graduated from college, was sitting in the dining room surrounded by her high school friends. The crowd was milling about, speaking in soft tones, making sincere and appropriate remarks as they gazed at the wall of family photographs. "Look at Denise skiing. Here she is when Allison was born." A moment later, the respectful, mournful mood was broken when the very attractive and divorced next-door neighbor strutted into the room carrying a homemade chocolate layer cake, and all heads turned. It was at precisely this moment—if it hadn't occurred to Stan, it certainly occurred to everyone in the room—that he wouldn't remain single forever.

Many widowers say they are still in mourning when the "casserole lady" or "brisket brigade" appears at their door. David laughs at the concept of a woman showing up bearing dinner. "I'd rather have one show up with a vacuum. I can cook!"

Alan says that exactly one week after he threw out his unfaithful wife, women in the neighborhood began calling him, asking him either directly or on behalf of a friend if he was ready to date. This isn't unusual, since most people aren't as sensitive to the timing issue with divorced men as they are with widowers. Especially in a case such as Alan's, where word quickly spread that his wife had cheated on him, the local single ladies were only too happy to soothe his pain.

So how do you deal with a casserole lady or nosy neighbor when you are still recovering from a death or divorce and are not ready to date? Politely thank her for the offer of food or help and then leave no door open, figuratively or literally. Try saying, "This is very kind of you. Everyone has been so wonderful to us. And we're doing as well as can be expected. Thank you." There is no need to invite her in. It may feel rude to conduct this conversation in your doorway, but it will help stymie any more-than-neighborly intentions. If, on the other hand, you find yourself attracted to this woman, consider several things before inviting her in to heat more than just the casserole. You've just lost a spouse; therefore your thinking is murky, your emotions are haywire, and your children are unprepared to see you with another woman. Accept the casserole by all means, but then close the door—at least for the time being.

So when should you begin dating? Is there an appropriate amount of time to wait after either separating from your wife or your spouse's death? Dr. Halpern says, "It's a very individual thing. You go through the various stages of grief after a death or divorce and then you move on. Some people are able to work through it sooner than others, and some people never get over it. My own experience for most people is it's somewhere between six months and a year to really process the loss and grieve."

Of course, that's a general timeline that is subject to your own circumstances. That neighbor who visited Stan? Several weeks later he went to thank her for the cake, and she told him to call if he needed anything. So a week later he "needed" a cup of sugar. (Well, not really, but why not?) The cup of sugar led to dinner out and, fast-forward a year, to an engagement. The neighbors may still not be over it.

Only Stan knew when he felt ready to move on and open himself up to a new love. He'll always love his first wife, but as any of us who've been through a death or divorce acutely realize, life is short. If you feel a connection with someone, you may not get a second chance.

One sign it's too early for you to begin dating, according to Dr. Halpern, is if you speak about your former wife frequently, whether in glowing or not-so-glowing terms. If you do, that's perfectly fine and normal, but hold off on dating for a while until you feel she's less present in your mind. You may even make a few false starts before you can get back in the race. I started dating about a year and a half after the death of my husband, Charlie. A couple of months and three different guys later, I abruptly stopped. I found myself avoiding dates and coming up with excuses to hang out with my kids. Some months later, once I'd had enough time to myself, it hit me: the loneliness, the desire to be touched, the yearning to go to dinner with someone besides my kids and at a place other than Friendly's. This time when I resumed dating, I was ready.

Testing the Waters

It has been a couple of months since your wife died and you're lying in bed fantasizing about being with an attractive coworker or neighbor. Is it heartless of you to be dreaming of another woman so soon? These feelings may both shame and excite you, but rest assured that they're completely normal. You're not yet ready to act on them, but the simple fact that you're having them serves as a positive sign that one day you'll unseal your heart and be open to loving someone new.

If an early relationship falls apart, it may be that you weren't really ready to begin dating. Alan, a forty-three-year-old firefighter, theorizes that "some guys come out of a divorce and forget that they are free. And there are others who are just driving down the street one day and it clicks—they can have a social life."

Drew knows he wasn't prepared to meet the first woman he dated. "She was lovely and smart," he says, "but I wasn't ready." After a few more dates with women who for one reason or another didn't appeal to him, he took some time off from the dating scene. "If someone's just getting out of a marriage, I'm not going to be their savior. I want to date a woman who's been out of a marriage for a while and is past the bitterness and into the optimism. I don't want to talk about somebody's ex-husband or my ex-wife. I don't want to plot with them. It's a dark, ugly side of you that comes out when you go through a divorce, and I don't want someone I've just met to see that in me."

Drew's right. Before you go on a date, you have to be past that stage, as do the women you meet. I once dated a divorced father who spent the entire meal not criticizing his ex-wife but praising her for "marrying up" (his phrase, not mine) the second time around. By the time our entrées arrived, I knew her name, her new husband's name, how much they'd paid for their new home, and where they were vacationing. I was gone before dessert.

Two years after his wife died, Gary invited a young woman from work over for dinner when his kids were away at camp. "She was way too young for me, but I felt it was time for me to start dating. We had a nice dinner and a glass of wine and started talking. I guess I scared her away with my talk about my late wife. She pretty much turned around and ran out the door. I took that first attempt as a sign that I wasn't ready, so I didn't go on another date for a while."

If a date doesn't go well, that doesn't mean you failed. Maybe she wasn't right for you, or maybe, like Gary, you just weren't ready. Dating the second time around is complicated. You're wondering if you still have it. You're fearful about whether you'll have difficulties performing in bed. You know your body isn't as svelte and buff as it once was. You're set in your ways. There's a consolation in this, though: she's probably worried about the exact same things.

Seth had put off dating for a couple of years after his wife died, focusing mainly on raising his kids. "I wasn't ready; there was so much to deal with. It took a lot of time to get through that. Could I even go through it again? Then I attended a couple of parties, and just being there made me realize how much I missed it. I'm testing the waters now. I've been with my kids all the time. I need some adult companionship."

Shortly before David and his wife divorced they moved to the East Coast from the Midwest. When his wife walked out on him and their children, he felt lost in a strange town with no friends. "My focus was my family. I didn't go out Friday night with the boys and shoot pool. I didn't have a support network; I had left mine in Chicago. And then all of a sudden, bam, here I am. I've got nothing."

So David joined a single parents group at his church, where he met a divorced mother of two. After a couple of brief conversations, he asked for her number, which she gave him on a business card that he carefully tucked into his shirt pocket. But when he returned home and faced the telephone, he realized that he wasn't ready to date. His feelings changed a few weeks later, but when he looked for the card, he discovered he had inadvertently laundered it with the shirt. He finally tracked her down through the Internet, and now they see each other once a week and talk every day.

Be prepared to fall into a few short-lived relationships before you hit your stride. Sometimes these early romances turn into something permanent and wonderful. But other times they get hold of you and drag you into a deep fog where it's difficult to distinguish your fear of being alone from your desire for genuine companionship. Force yourself to take a step back and process the situation. Is this a person with whom you *might* want to spend the rest of your life? Or is she merely filling the void your wife left behind? I understand how difficult it is to achieve this perspective. It's not as simple as when you were seventeen and dating a girl your parents didn't like. Now the decision is up to you, and any judgment you make affects not only your life and hers but the lives of your children and any she may have.

Sometimes the strains of life can cause you to plunge blindly into a new relationship rather than take a step back to assess the situation. Too many of us end up in atrocious relationships, even second marriages, because we're just too beleaguered to think straight. My daughter and I once nearly settled on an overpriced, shabby New York City apartment after being dragged around Manhattan all day long by a real estate agent. By 7:00 P.M. my feet hurt and my head throbbed. He gave me until 7:15 to make a decision. I felt pressured to find a place, and I didn't want to disappoint my daughter (who was more focused on being eight blocks from Central Park than on the holes in the walls opened to the elements), so I said yes. But before we signed anything, I took what little remaining energy I had and said, "I'm too tired to process this. Let me sleep on it." I did, my daughter did, and the next morning we saw clearly that we could do better. Breaking a rental lease is a snap compared to breaking up a serious relationship.

So sleep on it.

Honesty Is the Only Policy

A lot of fathers are afraid to tell their kids that they're dating for fear they'll respond horribly. David, for example, so agonizes over his daughter's anticipated reaction that he doesn't tell her when he is going on a date. Even when she sees him dressed up and asks where he is going, David only says, "Out with a friend." Let me explain something here: unless your children are homeschooled, watch no television, and spend their free time collecting butterflies, they know that when you say "out with a friend" without further elaboration, you are, in fact, meeting a woman. So just say, "I'm going out with a very nice woman I met through Uncle Joe." If you are genuinely worried about how your kids will react, this might not be the time to tell them that you met the woman online or in a bar. Allow them to deal first with the concept that you're dating. Details can follow after your child has had time to process and accept that Dad's social life now includes more than a Friday night poker game.

You should feel encouraged by the results of my survey, which found that even when you think your kids disapprove of your social life, you may be mistaken. Roughly half—49 percent—of the fathers say their kids are okay with their dating. Very few dads (only 16 percent) think their kids disapprove, and a substantial 35 percent say their kids won't even discuss the topic. Among the kids, three-quarters of them say they are fine with their dad's dating. The remaining 25 percent say either it's hard for them to accept or they outright don't like it.

Even when the kids' replies are categorized by age, the majority in each age group still claim to be fine with Dad's dating. Not surprisingly, the narrowest margin—though still a majority for acceptance—shows up in the difficult adolescent years of eleven to fourteen. Fifty-nine percent of those kids say they are okay with their father dating. For the young kids (ten and under), 71 percent are supportive, while 84 percent of teenagers (fifteen and older)—perhaps hoping that Dad will return the favor to them and extend their curfew—heartily approve of Dad's new social life. So, as much as you may be dreading this difficult conversation, remember that these statistics line up in your favor—your kids may be more supportive than you expect.

Gary is finally beginning to realize this. When he went on his first date, four years after losing his wife, he chose not to inform his kids. His eldest daughter, distressed over her mother's death, had threatened to harm herself so many times that he feared telling her might send her over the edge. Then one evening he and his girlfriend were eating dinner in a restaurant when they spotted a meddlesome neighbor across the room. Feeling as guilty as a kid caught with his hand in the cookie jar, they bailed out the back door. As if being a single father weren't tiring enough, Gary began furtively crafting stolen moments with his girlfriend: meeting at a secluded park, sneaking off to hotel rooms, and always lying to his daughters. He was worn out, and apparently so was his girlfriend—she grew weary of the subterfuge and ended the affair.

Gary next met a nurse at his youngest daughter's orthodontist's office, and this time decided to be honest with his kids. When he nervously told his eldest daughter he was going on a date, her response was a pleasant surprise. "Really?" she said. "That's great." Gary says, "When I told my other daughters that I had gone out with this nurse, my youngest one said, 'Cool. Is there going to be a second date?' It's unbelievable. I'm not sneaking around trees or popping out of manholes anymore."

You will feel an enormous sense of relief once you level

with your kids. Yes, they may react angrily or dramatically, or, as Gary found out, they may surprise you and be positive, even supportive. But the sooner you take this first step, the sooner your children will accept your new love life. They have two hurdles to overcome: one, as I mentioned earlier, is coming to terms with the fact that you and Mom will never again be a couple, and the other is to understand that a change in your social life will not alter your relationship with them. Before they can get past these obstacles, they may see their lives as so out of their control that the only way to regain some small portion of that control is to make *your* life difficult.

Ben didn't tell his children about his girlfriend until he invited her over for dinner. To his amazement, they weren't angry that he had begun dating, but they were deeply hurt that he had concealed his relationship from them for months. It's the fear of the unknown that provokes our kids' worst nightmares. It's not the fact that you're dating, it's the consequences of it. Think Cinderella and the wicked stepmother. If you fall for some woman, will you forget about them? Will they have to move? Will they have to change schools? Will there be evil stepsisters as well? Will you spend so much money on this new woman that you won't be able to take them to Disney World like you promised? The list is endless. If they feel you have been honest all along regarding your social life, they will be less fearful of these possible changes. They might even think that, in the end, your choices will benefit them as well.

For years, eighteen-year-old Mike's father kept his love life a secret from his kids. "My dad didn't tell me he was dating, but I kind of figured he might be," Mike says. "After my parents separated he seemed to discover this whole new side of himself. He went out to parties. One night he came back to the house with this gaggle of women and it was really bizarre. I felt as though it was a little inappropriate for him to do. But it allowed me to see a different side of him and his existence. I wouldn't have admitted it then, but I was angry and certainly surprised. I also found the women he brought back to be personally unattractive. I didn't like the kind of people they were. I was more unimpressed that these were the people he wanted to spend time with than the fact that he was dating. I didn't say anything to him, and he didn't say anything to me, either."

More than two years passed after that evening, and Mike's father still had not discussed dating with his son. Then one day out of the blue, he introduced Mike to a woman who, as it turned out, he had been seriously involved with for two years and who would be moving in with them. The news rattled Mike, who says he would have been okay with it if the subject of his father's dating had ever arisen. But the fact that his dad had remained so evasive eroded any trust Mike had in him. What else was he concealing? Who was this woman who knew his father so well? Mike has since moved in with his mother.

"My take on my dad hiding his dates from me for two years is that it is much better to be up-front and open about the whole thing than to keep it from anyone," Mike says. "As soon as his personal behavior became secretive he essentially made everyone feel as though he'd betrayed them. Everything would have been better if he had been honest from the start."

And don't wait for your child to broach the subject. As Ben learned, it's your job to bring it up, and the longer you wait, the more upset they'll be when they find out. You only need to mention it casually, though; if your kids want details, they'll ask.

Forty-eight-year-old Warren tells his kids that anytime they want to talk about his love life, he's happy to discuss it. "But I don't go out of my way," he says. "I don't press the issue, and they don't bring it up." His children are aware their father is dating and appreciate his open communication, but they aren't yet ready to hear more about his girlfriends. "They feel a little uncomfortable because they think I'm uncomfortable talking about my dating, but I'm really not."

Dr. Halpern's advice is to begin a conversation with something like this: " 'I love you. We have a nice life together, but I am at a point where I need adult companionship.' " He recommends saying that in addition to the wonderful relationship you have with them and all of the great friends you have, you also want the kind of relationship you can only have between a man and a woman. "With little kids, tell them you need someone who will be a good friend and with whom you can do things. With teens you can talk about intimacy without going into details of sexuality," he says. "Kids will often respond by saying, 'But you have us. And you have your male friends.' Tell them that you need the type of intimacy and affection you once had with their mom. With teens you can add, 'It's the kind of thing you'll understand better when you start having girlfriends and boyfriends,' and the kids who are dating usually get it right away. *Intimacy* is the code word."

Always try to speak with them face-to-face. It's too easy to bring up the topics you dread while driving your kids to band practice or ballet class. I'm guilty of this. But the frenzy of the outside world and your kids' anxiousness about not wanting to be late fosters a distracted environment and a passive response from your child. He might even say "Sure, that's cool" just to get it over with, which you could mistakenly perceive as acceptance or agreement.

If you are widowed, you will have to explain to your children that the fact that you're dating in no way means you will forget or stop loving their mother. While ten-year-old Sarah is trying to understand her father's dating, her fourteen-year-old sister, Nancy, is much more conflicted. She thinks her father no longer cares about her mother, who died when she was ten. "Dating is like he's trying to get over her death, like he's trying to forget," Nancy says. "I don't understand why he has to begin dating. I like it just the three of us." Explain to your children that love expands. That is how you were always able to love their mother and sister and brother simultaneously without loving any one family member less than another. Be sensitive to the fact that while your kids probably have difficulty talking about their mom, they will be devastated if you seem to remove her from your lives. Don't refrain from speaking about their mom or bringing up happy memories.

Warren discovered that even if you try to keep your social life a secret, your kids have a way of finding out. He hadn't told his children about a woman he'd been dating for five months when he took his nine-year-old son and his friends to the beach one Sunday knowing the woman would be there. They arranged to say hello when they went to buy ice cream. "We walked past her. I said hi and introduced her to my son. I didn't say who she was. Later he said to me, 'Dad, is that your girlfriend?' I was flummoxed."

Sarah realizes her dad kept the news of his dating from her and her sister because he didn't want to upset them. "But it kind of hurt that he would be keeping it from us," she explains. "Sometimes it can turn out worse if the dad isn't honest and doesn't tell the kids."

You must open up judgment-free dialogue with your kids even if they act unreceptive at first. Eventually they'll hear you. It's always better that they learn about your love life from you rather than from your ex-wife. If, for example, your kids don't like the woman you're seeing and think they can't talk about her with you, they may choose to confide in their mother instead. Wouldn't you rather hear it directly from your kids? Anytime your ex-wife has an opportunity to offer her opinion on your relationship, she may influence your kids and further isolate them from you.

Also keep in mind that your ex-wife may discuss her social life with your kids from the outset, causing you to appear deceitful if you wait to do so. Fifteen-year-old Justin says his mother confessed to dating long before his dad did. As a result, he and his siblings believe that while their mom cares what they think, their father doesn't. Compounding the problem is that they don't discuss their feelings with their dad, and so he just assumes everything is fine. "He thinks that we can handle it all," Justin says. "He's always saying, 'You guys are great.' We hear it all the time. He assumes we're cool with everything, and he shouldn't because sometimes we're not."

You want so fervently to believe your children are doing fine that you may fail to recognize the worries that lie beneath the surface. We're all guilty of this sometimes. As single parents, we are handling so much that if we can eliminate any issues, we are more than happy to indulge ourselves. Find those quieter moments, maybe at lunch on a Saturday or in the evening when you are tucking them in, to tell them, "I know you have been dealing with a lot, and I thank you for putting up with me. I'm inexperienced as a single parent, and I can't always tell if I should be doing something differently. Promise me you'll tell me if you think I should." Reinforce with your children that if they'd feel more comfortable talking to another adult—a therapist, school counselor, or close family friend—that is always available to them. Continue to offer them this option because their feelings about counseling will change from time to time and you want to make it available when it is desired.

Tom's father made a point of involving his son before he began dating, and the trust that resulted between the two of them has been invaluable. Following the death of his mother, Tom's family would get together with his mom's best friend and her kids. It felt natural and relaxed. Both sets of kids had grown up together and knew the parents on a first-name basis. Then one day his father asked him if it would be okay if he dated this woman. At first, Tom was shocked and upset that his father would consider dating after his mom had died. But as Tom began to appreciate that his father had asked him first, he gave his dad his wholehearted approval.

I understand that certain circumstances may make it difficult to tell your kids about a woman you're seeing, especially if it doesn't appear the relationship will last. You might date a close girlfriend of your former wife or even a family friend, as Tom's dad did, and because the kids have known her for years and may be close to her, the relationship might be too complex for them to handle. If you get involved with this woman they already care about and then break up, it may be devastating to lose yet another mother figure. Jim understands this, and although he has been honest with his daughters about the other women he's dated, he never told them about dating his ex-wife's best friend. If this on-again, off-again relationship ever appears to be heading someplace serious, he knows he will have to tell them.

It's also possible that you could begin seeing your ex-wife again. Your kids should see the two of you being cordial with one another, but you don't want to get their hopes up. If you are really uncertain as to whether you will end up back together, just let your children know that you and Mom are still good friends. Let's face it, regardless of how guarded your comments are, your kids will never stop wishing for a reconciliation.

Quality Time

There is a distinction between being a father and being a dad. A father merely produces a child, but a dad nourishes one. Of course, you know this already. Even though you have every intention of dating and falling in love again, your children's health and happiness are your first priority. Sometimes our children witness us so wrapped up in a new social life that they don't always see this. Dr. Halpern's advice is to make sure you schedule time specifically for them. Quality time, as clichéd as that term is, will make your kids feel important and confident that you're making an effort to be together. Reaffirm with them that regardless of whether you meet a new woman, your role as their dad will never change. For these kids who have been through a death or divorce, abandonment is a real fear.

The single-parent experience will probably bring you even closer to your child. The kids I interviewed all say their bond with their dad intensified after their parents' marriage ended. If you think they do not comprehend the physical and emotional strain you are under as a single dad, you aren't giving them enough credit. They want to help you; they just don't always know how.

Listen to nineteen-year-old Daniel, who says, "When

my mom died of cancer, I was too young to fully grasp her illness. Everyone had high hopes that she was improving—she no longer had her hair, but she had that glow. I went away to camp, and when I came back home her condition had deteriorated. My memories of my dad prior to my mom's illness were that he worked a lot, even on the weekends. His presence wasn't strong at all. But after she died, my relationship with him completely changed. I remember every time he had to do one of her chores he'd say it was hard, so I helped out by making dinner a lot—Velveeta, noodles, chicken, french fries. I just grew closer to him, especially after my brother left for school. We really bonded. He is the male role model that has kept me balanced."

Seventeen-year-old Christine says her mother had always taken the primary parenting role in her family. Strong-willed just like her dad, Christine was apprehensive about whether she and her father would get along after her mother died. Her older brother moved back home to help his dad take care of his sisters. "I felt bad that he had to assume that role and my dad wasn't going to," she says. Only fourteen at the time, Christine had a difficult time adjusting to life with Dad, who was unprepared to raise a feisty teenage daughter by himself. "Mom had parented and Dad had worked. I'm a girl, so he was totally lost," she explains. "Then, when he began dating I blew up. Our relationship hit the fan."

The bond between a father and child often feels strained when neither one is comfortable articulating feelings. This can improve in two ways: one is with patience (all kids grow up eventually), and the other is by eliminating any reason your child has to doubt your love. In Christine's case, both of these occurred. As she packed her bags for college, she looked back on the tumultuous years she'd had with her father and acknowledged that despite it all, a close bond had developed out of their caring for and depending on each other.

You may be going through a trying time now with a son or daughter whose defiance or opposition to your new social life is really a consequence of being overcome by the loss of a mother, whether through death or divorce. Kids need your understanding since they may not realize what's causing their anger or how to resolve it. They know they are making your life miserable; they just don't know how else to cope. Nancy admits she has given her dad a hard time since her mother died. She is frequently truant from school and constantly threatens to run away. She recognizes how challenging it is for her dad to parent by himself. Her father won't give up on her, and slowly, with the help of therapy and his unconditional support, she's making some progress.

Whatever you do, don't burden your kids with any insecurities you might be experiencing as a result of being single again. Forty-nine-year-old Drew inadvertently puts pressure on his child by playing the "rejected" spouse. Now that his wife is happily remarried, he admits he enjoys the attention and sympathy he gets because he's not currently in a relationship. Being a martyr is unfair to your kids and to yourself. Children are pained when one parent seems dejected and doesn't date while the other is happily coupled. How can they ever heal from a divorce if they think one of their parents is still suffering? Drew admits that he'd love to be with a woman, but for now he tells his son he doesn't have to share Daddy with anyone. It's not a matter of sharing, however. If you have more than one child, it's doubtful that they think they have to share you with their siblings. You're one unit that's made up of individual lives, and the amount of time you spend together ebbs and flows quite naturally. It's the same way when you begin dating. Just as you don't skip back-to-school night because you have a date, you also don't sit home eating leftover pizza and watching *Dirty Harry* for the umpteenth time while your daughter goes to a sleepover. If you are there for your child on the "ordinary days," as Warren describes, then you'll raise a house full of happy adults—and that includes you.

Only recently has fifty-nine-year-old Nick begun to understand this. His son had been struggling with his parents' divorce, so Nick tried his best to be an involved dad. He rented an apartment three blocks away from where his son and daughter lived with their mother. He'd take the red-eye back from his West Coast business trips so he could attend his children's games and other events in their lives. But it wasn't until his son left for college that he knew his efforts had registered with his kids. When he dropped him off at his freshman dorm, his son turned to him and said, "You've been a great dad. The only thing you haven't done as a parent was tuck me in at night."

As difficult as it is to raise children alone, for many men—like Jason—their kids are also their salvation. Jason was so depressed after Cynthia died that he struggled to get dinner on the table. His kids would come home from school and find an empty refrigerator. It never occurred to him to defrost the food in the freezer. Even when he lost twenty pounds he wasn't aware his kids had noticed. Then one evening when he came home from the office, his son walked in behind him carrying a bag of take-out food. Talk about a value meal. "Tears just rolled down my cheeks," Jason says. That night his kids decided to take turns providing dinner.

Don't run yourself ragged trying to be perfect. As Jason discovered, you don't need to prepare a gourmet dinner to spend quality time with your kids. Once you reach a balance as a single parent—being involved and responsible without creating unrealistic expectations for yourself—you'll find time to enjoy a much-needed social life. It's about how you connect with your kids. As children, they will always want and need your attention, even if they act ambivalent or contrary. They fear that you'll forget about them as soon as you meet another woman. Although you know this isn't the case, your children may need to be reminded.

Ben goes out of his way to pay attention to his youngest son. Only twelve, his son dreaded the day his older siblings would move out of the house and leave him behind. "My goal was to make sure he got a lot of the attention," says Ben. "I feel bad about the divorce in the first place. I worry about him. I want to make sure he has every opportunity that I had, that his older brothers had. I still feel guilty."

Incidentally, though they can be a great help during this time, older kids need and deserve the same consideration as their younger siblings. Involving them doesn't mean taking advantage of their age by asking them to babysit so you can go on a date. If you would like their help with child care now and then, let them offer, and then pay them fairly. They are giving up time with their most crucial support system—their friends—to help you out. Don't put your children in Nancy's position. Her father's girlfriend asks her to babysit her daughter as well as Nancy's younger sister. "I can't say no," Nancy says. "There would be an argument." Her dad doesn't realize that this makes his daughter uncomfortable. He erroneously thinks placing all the kids together bonds them like a family. Since, like Nancy, most older kids won't tell you how they really feel about such requests, make it a point to ask them.

In the absence of a spouse, it is also very tempting to confide in our older children about serious issues such as problems at work or financial concerns. While they may be flattered that you trust them with this information, it will affect them deeply. They deserve the opportunity to experience their childhood without the added burden of adult responsibilities. Those will come soon enough!

Breaking News: Dad Is Dating! 47

Whatever Makes You Happy

As parents, we often say we just want our kids to be happy. That wish is the natural order of things. What we may not realize is that our children want the same for us, though they seldom verbalize it. If a child is the product of a conventional family with two healthy parents at the helm, he has no need to contemplate his parents' contentment. But when a child has a single mother or father, he becomes much more attuned to that parent's emotions. When you lose your partner, you become vulnerable in ways your children haven't seen before. They now notice and are affected by your ups and downs. What they all want is for you to be happy. And if that means your falling in love with another woman, your kids know that ultimately they will learn to accept it.

Christine has butted heads with her father ever since her mother died. Picturing her dad with another woman is unacceptable to her. But now that she's leaving for college, the thought of him being alone is unbearable. "I want him to be happy, totally. I can be self-centered all I want, but what does that do for anybody? As uncomfortable as it is for me, it's not about me. He has half his life left. It's hard to meet someone in your fifties. I know that. But he can't be alone. He wouldn't survive."

Tracey values her parents' happiness. They divorced when she was only four. In her twenties now, she can look back and admit that the breakup was for the best. Both her mother and her father have remarried. "I'm happy that they are both in relationships because I don't want them to be alone. I want them to be happy."

None of this minimizes how difficult it will be for your children to see you with another woman, but time and exposure to her will help that. As your children mature, they will appreciate that your new relationship makes you happy. Young Sarah admits it's really difficult for her to see her father with another woman since her mother died, but she says she gets over her dismay when "I see my dad smile. 'Cause I haven't seen him smile like that in a long time."

———

Now that you are a single father, your relationship with your children has changed. You, and they, will never again take it for granted. They know how difficult your life has become, and they want to help, even if they don't show it. They understand that you deserve a social life, even if witnessing it is upsetting for them. And, most of all, they want you to be happy, even if it takes years for you to realize it.

2

Dating 101

I could tell instantly when my son discovered girls. One day he unceremoniously replaced his posters of Michael Jordan and Wayne Gretzky with Katie Holmes and the Olsen twins, and when he ran to catch his school bus, the pungent odor of cologne trailed behind him like a startled teenage skunk.

You remember those days—when dating meant covering up your acne, showing off your wit in front of the freckle-faced girl in algebra class, and earning enough money from mowing lawns or bagging groceries that you could buy a used car. And not just any used car, but one that, even if it broke down with some frequency, elevated your cool factor. Dating was easier years ago for two reasons: you knew where to meet girls, and you weren't all that concerned with what your family thought of them.

But today, as a single father, you will find that meeting women requires a little more creativity. And although your parents won't influence your choice, your children will.

Your kids fear that some conniving woman will cast her spell over you, bewitching you into forsaking your role as their dad. And your kids, according to Dr. Halpern, might not be too far off the mark. Some men become so distracted while pursuing a romantic relationship that they unintentionally fail to address the needs of their children. "These are the men who begin dating and believe the kids can handle themselves," he says.

They can't. They still need you. And while you may think you are giving them enough attention (and you probably are), the minute you begin dating they see you as unavailable. Sarah and Nancy's dad can't win. He comes home from work every night to make dinner, do the housework, and help his kids with homework. But when he's ready to have some time for himself on the weekend, his daughters disapprove. "He moves too fast," insists Nancy. "He's already spent more money on his ex-girlfriend than I think he spent on us. They were only seeing each other three weeks. I don't like the fact that he spent all his time with her and left me with my sister. I say, 'You're the parent. I'm the kid. You are supposed to be home taking care of your other daughter, not me.' He says he is allowed to go out once in a while. But every weekend?"

Like it or not, all children—like Nancy—have a way of influencing your social life. Not only is a relationship affected by their opinion of the woman, but she, too, will assess you in part by how she regards your kids. Long gone is that boy judged entirely on his looks, charisma, and car.

Decoding Women:
Finnegans Wake Is an Easier Read

While the most notable change in dating, now that you're a single dad, will be the presence of your kids, be aware that another aspect has *not* changed very much: women. They (okay, we) are still hard to satisfy. We want you to be perfect yet humble, sensitive yet manly, good-looking yet modest. And we want you to effortlessly decipher our every need, want, and desire without any direction from us.

We know this about ourselves and sometimes we kid about it woman to woman. Let me share a joke circulating among us on the Internet. A group of women go to a store to buy a husband. As they climb higher through the store the men's attributes increase. The women can go up but they can't go down except to exit the building. Floor one has men with jobs. Floor two has men with jobs who love kids. By the time they get to the fifth floor, the men have jobs, love kids, are drop-dead handsome, like housekeeping, and are great lovers. Still not satisfied, the women head to the sixth and final floor, where a sign greets them: "You are visitor number 31,345,012. There are no men on this floor. It exists solely as proof that women are impossible to please."

Wait, there's more! Across the street is a similar store for men looking for wives. The first floor has wives who love sex; the second has wives who love sex and have money. The third through sixth floors have never been visited.

It's not that each gender looks for entirely dissimilar attributes, but women and men prioritize these attributes differently (remember, good looks are first on the list for men and down at number six for women). What you need to know about women is that regardless of their age and their emotional and financial independence, they still crave attention and adoration from you. How do you do that? Remember when you pulled up to your friend's house in your new convertible and after compulsively locking it three times, you turned to sneak an admiring look at that beauty on the street? You should look at your girlfriend the same way. Women pick up on these subtleties and, more important, so do their friends.

Incidentally, this is the same reason they prefer jewelry from you more than almost any other gift. It's not the expense or their need to amass a treasure chest; it's the only sort of present they can show off repeatedly by wearing it to work, to church, or to the grocery store, which means other women will almost certainly comment, "I like your necklace." To which your girlfriend can proudly respond, "Sam gave it to me."

Here's another lesson in your crash course in women: as a way to gain insight into you, women will check out your shoes. Are they rich Italian leather or scruffy sneakers? One says you're having wine with dinner, the other says a six-pack. (Incidentally, if you think a particular shoe looks good with a suit, then don't wear it with jeans, and vice versa. Safe bet all around: loafers.)

As you become more experienced with dating again,

you'll begin to recognize the signs that a woman likes you. But for starters, know that if she doesn't return your call—even though at the end of the evening she said, "I'd love to get together again"—cut your losses and move on.

If you really like her, after an initial meeting do not ask her out for Sunday lunch or, worse yet, a weeknight. She wants, and expects, to be your date on Saturday night. Women put a lot of emphasis on the night of the week. It's the difference between sitting on the bench and being in the starting lineup.

If you go back to her house after dinner and she offers you coffee and cake, take note where it's being served. The kitchen table says, "Thank you for dinner." The sofa says, "I hope you told your babysitter to stay late."

All kidding about the husband store aside, women want a man they can respect and trust, and who respects and trusts them as well. We all should demand no less as we begin to date.

Blind Luck

If no hot (her, not the dish) casserole lady ever showed up at your door you're probably wondering how to meet women. There are many dating venues, from the Internet to dating services to activity clubs, but the most time-honored of all is the blind date fix-up. Single women generally prefer fix-ups to nearly all other ways of meeting men, while single guys tend to get a little panicky about these introductions—especially if they're told, "She's got a great personality." Men fear that they'll open the door to a woman who, though she might be the life of the party, might closely resemble the Wicked Witch of the West.

Conrad and Jason both had had terrible blind dates in the past. Jason says that as a result, he became wary every time someone said a girl was perfect for him. Conrad insists that each of his blind dates was such a disaster that eventually he begged his friends to stop setting him up.

Don't be too quick to dismiss blind dates. Even if the woman isn't Eva Longoria, a friend of a friend is more of a known quantity than a nameless stranger you'd meet in a bar. So don't be reluctant to tell your friends, family, and coworkers that you are willing to be introduced to someone. They'll essentially prescreen your dates for you, which, as Robert discovered, reduces some of the anxiety about meeting strangers. A high school teacher in a small town, he prefers to meet women through friends rather than showing up at singles bars or inadvertently connecting with a former student online. His current long-term girlfriend was a fix-up.

Another advantage to fix-ups is that these dates are the easiest to explain to your children. Your kids will be a little more accepting and less threatened if the woman you go out with came to you by way of someone they know and trust. They may also think that you weren't actively trying to date and it is out of politeness that you agreed to meet this woman. How noble of you.

If you are truly nervous about going on a blind date, ask your friend for the woman's e-mail address or phone number and spend some time getting to know her before meeting in person. If you feel you are connecting during this reconnaissance, you might actually put less emphasis on her less-than-movie-star looks when you finally meet. Gary was set up with a woman with whom he developed an e-mail correspondence before they got together. "I sent her an e-mail that took me a day to write even though it was very brief. I kept it kind of short because I wasn't sure how much to incriminate myself in it. She responded with a book."

Gary was smart to keep his first e-mail relatively short. As you continue to correspond, your e-mails will become more detailed. Don't give away information that is better explained in person, such as the reason for your divorce or the problems your middle child is facing in school. And be aware that e-mails don't always reflect the tone you are trying to convey and can easily be misinterpreted. Reread what you've written before hitting the send button to make sure your periods, exclamation points, and question marks are suitably placed. You can e-mail her your picture if you'd like, which should automatically invite her to do the same.

Making It on Your Own

If you're saying, "No brisket lady. No fix-ups. How do I meet women on my own?" take some advice from Dr. Halpern, who encourages the men he counsels to meet women through pursuing activities they enjoy. "Go out and join clubs or groups. Doing something that you like to do is attractive to women. Don't pick fillers; pick things that you genuinely like so you will meet someone who shares your interests and passions. You're going to stumble and fumble your way through some disappointments, but if you want a meaningful relationship in your life, sometimes you have to go out and find it."

Bars and clubs—you remember them from the days when your evening began rather than ended at 11:00 P.M.—are still places to meet women. Offering to buy an attractive woman a drink hasn't lost its appeal now that you actually hope the bartender *will* card you and the drink isn't served in a can. Forget the old pickup lines, though, such as "What do you like for breakfast?" It's not cute or retro, just extremely uncool. Take your mother's advice and simply be yourself. Start with: "Hi. This place is really busy tonight." "Yes, it sure is lively," she'll say. And if she doesn't turn her back on you or gaze past your shoulder toward some guy shooting pool, then introduce yourself. If she continues to stay engaged in direct eye contact with you, take that as a good sign and offer to buy her a drink. After that, you're on your own.

Not all men are comfortable going to bars to meet women. Conrad prefers being someplace with people of similar backgrounds. Approaching a woman in a bar, he says, was easier when he was in his twenties and surrounded by his friends. Dwight agrees. "I can't just walk up to them," he says. "I have to share some link to them other than standing next to the same bar. I have to experience them somewhere else in life. I've been attracted to people that either I worked with or that I knew from high school or previous jobs. I'm never very good with strangers."

Dwight ended up reuniting with an ex-girlfriend when he ran into her at a high school reunion. The two began dating six months after his wife died, and they stayed together for three years. When he went to his next five-year reunion, he met another woman. Today the two of them have built a house and are living together.

Examining your day-to-day activities a little more closely often reveals prospective dates, too. If Gary hadn't taken his daughter to her orthodontist that day, he never would have met the nurse. When she told his daughter, "I like your hair. Did your mom do it?" (single women are pretty sharp, guys), Gary explained he was widowed. "I'm so sorry," she said, pretending to read his daughter's file. On the drive home, his daughter said, "Dad, you were flirting with her." A week later when they returned for a follow-up appointment, Gary wrote his name and number on a Post-it note and surreptitiously slipped it to the nurse when his daughter wasn't looking. She called him that evening.

Despite the chance the nurse would have ignored his note, Gary realized it was a risk worth taking. Six months later they were still going strong. If you want to be in a relationship, sometimes you have to be assertive. Go after dating with an energy that says, *I'm attractive, worthwhile, and entitled to be romantically involved.* Take a lesson from Ben, who describes himself as "driven." He says, "I'm not going to sit back and wait. I've never sat back and waited for things to happen. I pursue what I want."

Gary met someone because his daughter needed braces. You've got kids, too, so use them! Figure out ways to participate in their school activities: chaperone parties and school trips, attend their games and school plays, offer to bring punch or cups for the Halloween party and then hang around with the other parents. You will find that you are mostly among women, married or single, who will be delighted to have your company. Even if they aren't single, they might have friends who are. And your kids will be so appreciative of your attention and involvement, you can't lose.

Look for hidden opportunities to meet women in places you might not normally consider. Instead of grabbing an espresso to go, linger for a while at your local coffee shop. Bring something that is a conversation starter and have a seat. If you have a young child, take him with you and get him a special treat. Women won't be able to resist talking to him. If not, bring a book (heck, bring this one if you really want to cut to the chase) or a newspaper so she can comment on a provocative title or headline, or a magazine, such as *Wired* or *Rolling Stone*, that reflects your interests. You might end up meeting a fellow computer geek or scheduling a date for an upcoming concert.

Your local supermarket—even for those who rank grocery shopping just below a trip to the proctologist—is a hot spot for meeting singles. If you notice a woman with an empty ring finger heading into the salad dressing aisle, feign ignorance and ask her if she can make a recommendation. Is there really a difference between honey mustard and honey Dijon? What exactly is balsamic vinaigrette? Has she ever been to that restaurant down the street that makes delicious salads? She's never been? You'd be happy to take her there for lunch sometime.... If you are an epicurean, don't be reluctant to offer your unsolicited advice to an attractive woman. Maybe you can steer her to the right wine to match the cheese in her cart or, if you overhear her ordering from the butcher, recommend a great way to grill that New York strip.

While the supermarket offers a lot of conversation starters, nothing compares with your pooch. In terms of your social life, a dog is truly man's best friend. If a woman sees you walking that adorable mutt, she'll stop to pet him—and talk to you. If you don't have a pet, borrow a friend's and take it to the park for the day, or volunteer at the local humane society as a dog walker. It's win-win for all three of you. In some cities, you can actually lease a dog for a weekend or longer—canine companionship without responsibility!

There are also many organizations that cater to singles. Conrad belongs to a local one for middle-aged single people. The group gets together every two to four weeks for dinner at someone's home and has already produced two marriages. Singles groups of all sorts—from religious to single-parenting-related—are listed in your local newspaper, online, and in the yellow pages.

Other places to meet women might involve a little culture or healthy activity. Many art museums offer singles nights. You can focus your attention on the Salvador Dalí and then humbly admit out loud that you don't get it. By doing so, you're encouraging that woman nearby to comment. If she wanders to the next painting with you, she just might be interested in more than the artwork. If you are athletic, sports and activity clubs such as ones for skiing, biking, and hiking are great places to meet women, even if they aren't specifically marketed to singles. Sign up for a charity race, join a local coed volleyball league, or hang out at the driving range or batting cages at the park. Chances are some single women have come there in search of you, too. Even if you don't meet your perfect match, you'll be with like-minded people while making some new friends and getting in shape.

Singles events often take place in churches and synagogues, restaurants, and theaters and are worth checking out. Look online and in your local newspaper for fun things to do, such as wine tastings or cooking classes, or volunteer to help at a local library, children's museum, or zoo. Think of places frequented by the single women you'd like to meet (participate, for example, in the March of Dimes Walk or Race for the Cure).

Travel clubs for singles have become more popular as tour operators capitalize on the number of single people who are looking for company when they travel. You can find these trips in magazine ads, from a travel agent, or online. You might check out Match.com, which offers online booking for singles trips on the travel section of their Web site. If you can afford a family vacation with your children, then go on an organized tour. A travel agent can tell you which ones attract single-parent families.

Surfing USA

By now you've heard the horror stories about the Internet: everyone lies; you never know who you'll meet; there are a lot of crazies. Yet you'll hook up with someone you just met in a bar? Really, meeting a date online is much less risky than the trip you and your high school buddies are planning to Vegas—even though they're both crapshoots.

If you're concerned about what your children will think, remember that the Internet to them is as routine as sharing one phone line was for you growing up. In fact, the sites your kids use to connect with their friends are far more revealing and provocative than any dating site you might visit. Reassure them that before you meet any of these women, you will check their profiles and communicate with them through e-mail or by phone. As tempting as it may be, don't share a woman's profile with your kids. You're looking to develop a relationship between two adults. Any woman you meet deserves that respect.

Internet dating is immediate. You want to connect with someone tonight? Go on one of the plethora of dating sites and browse. If someone piques your interest, then sign up for the site. You could conceivably have a date for the weekend. The number of baby boomer singles—born between 1946 and 1964—who visit online dating sites has grown every year. Match.com, the most well-known dating site since its creation in 1995, says people over the age of fifty make up its fastest-growing user demographic, a 300 percent increase since 2000. Yahoo! Personals finds that age bracket makes up 21 percent of the visitors to their site. And although men are typically more comfortable with the Internet, which makes it top-heavy with them, in the general population, there are 1.4 single women of baby boomer age (that's roughly early forties to mid-sixties, if you haven't done the math yet) for every male baby boomer, or a total of nearly sixteen million single women.

With numbers like these, should you really be reluctant to go online? David admits that despite the fact that he's a "real high-tech guy," the last thing he wants to do is join an Internet dating site. "I'm terrified my ex-wife will make fun of it," he says. It's not like she doesn't know he's single. Going online doesn't mean you're lacking in dates; it simply means you are wisely availing yourself of every avenue possible to meet a woman. If I were David's ex-wife, I would actually feel a little intimidated if I read a flattering profile of him online.

If you want to try online dating, log on to a particular Web site (see the chart at the end of this section) and the site's instructions will guide you along. Most allow you to browse a series of profiles before you even sign up. Once you do, you'll be asked to fill out your own profile and submit a photo. On average it costs about $25 a month, depending on the site. The advantage of the bigger sites is that they have huge databases. The disadvantage is that huge databases make it more difficult to pinpoint someone whose personality closely matches yours. The more specialized sites, such as RightStuffDating.com, which caters to graduates of top colleges, or Nerve.com, whose clientele largely consists of edgy, sexy urban singles looking for less serious relationships, have smaller but more select data-bases.

If you find it difficult to write a profile about yourself, then ask a friend for help. Drew got together with a female friend and each wrote the other one's profile and took each other's picture. "With all due modesty, I'm very good-looking—a poor man's Paul Newman," he says, so he felt less conceited asking a friend to compose his profile.

You often hear that people lie in their profiles. Some small embellishments are usually harmless, but lying about your age, for example, or using a twenty-year-old photo is pointless. You'll meet someone in person and she'll never want to see you again, and you'll go through the re-jection of wondering why she wasn't interested. Also, some sites have a system whereby users can give feedback on their dates and rank them. If you aren't honest, you won't rank very well. Plus, you don't want your profile on Dontdatehimgirl.com. The one exception I make to my honesty rule is for height. If you want to add an inch or two (you didn't hear that from me), go right ahead. Some women plug in "over five foot eight" on their require-ments, and if you are shorter than that, you won't appear on their radar screen. For years I've been telling such women they're missing out on the Michael J. Foxes of the world. If you've got the rest of the package, more likely than not they'll be interested.

A few words about the photo: skip the ones from your high school yearbook, any picture that features your mother, the ones that show your arm extending over a phantom woman who's been excised from the picture, and those in which you're embracing a car with a caption that says "my one and only." (Really, some guys do this.) Post something current and attractive that showcases you doing something fun, such as rock climbing, surfing, or playing with your dog. It's appealing to a woman to see that a man has many interests and is active.

The idea of using the Internet for dating unnerves Warren, who says, "You can't judge someone's honesty and integrity in a virtual environment. People misrepresent themselves. They lie about themselves. I don't entirely blame them, because you want to put your best foot forward. But you meet them and they are nothing like who they say they are." That can happen, and if you meet a lot of women online, it definitely will happen to you at least once. But just because you are meeting a woman in person—say, at a bar—rather than online doesn't necessarily mean you are being fed the truth about her, either. People's life stories always come from a very biased source—themselves.

Ben says he told the truth in his online profile. "I said that if I lived in Nottingham Forest I would have been Robin Hood. I dress like Columbo and I have the personality of MacGyver. I'm not going to attract a high-society type of woman. I was brutally honest because I'm not a venture capitalist and I don't have a huge home. If that's what you want, I'm not right for you." That kind of honesty is refreshing to women.

I tell women not to expect perfect dates. Neither should you. You will be disappointed over and over again. Ben signed up for eHarmony.com, a Web site that matches people based on the answers they provide to an extensive personality profile. "It was 100 percent not for me," he says. "I don't know what I was looking for, quite honestly. A Hollywood model with a genius IQ? After one date I didn't see the perfect thing, which is absolutely ridiculous, of course. After five or six of these dates I crashed and burned. I didn't want to do it anymore."

Fortunately, Alan never got to that point. He found success on JDate.com, a site for Jewish singles. Forty at the time, he searched for women between the ages of thirty-five and forty-five in his southern city and got more than five hundred hits. "I met some lovely people," he says. "There was only one person I couldn't wait to get away from, and she wasn't who she said she was." But Alan persisted and three weeks later, he saw a new listing that intrigued him. "We met for coffee, and it was great. We were there for two hours. We discovered we're only two months apart in age and have an amazing number of similarities." Today, Alan and his sweetheart.com are married.

There are also many Internet sites that, for a fee, will help guide you through the process of online dating. Some of those include:

TRUEDATER.COM	If you're concerned about whether a woman's profile is truthful, this site will check into her background. From the entire pool of online relationship seekers, it claims to weed out 5 percent with criminal convictions and another 5 percent who are already married.
DATESMART.COM	They do private investigations and confidential background verification checks dedicated to personal relationships. Rather than submit a request online, this site requires you to speak to someone by phone in order to create a personalized, confidential plan.
ROMANCESCAM.COM	This is a database of known scammers who first establish a friendly e-mail relationship and then claim something tragic, such as having a sick child in need of an operation, and ask you for money. These scammers usually swipe a photo from a model's Web site in order to attract your attention. Imagine that first meeting.
PROFILEHELPER.COM	After you fill out their questionnaire, they will create a profile you can use on dating sites. For an additional fee— about $150—you can also speak directly to a dating advisor for help with your profile.

PERSONALSTRAINER.COM	As with the other profile sites, they will write a profile based on the questionnaire you fill out. For $300, you can also choose to be advised by a private "personals" trainer who is a noted Internet dating relationship expert.
E-CYRANO.COM	This site also will help you rewrite a profile or create a new one. In either case, you will spend some time talking by phone to an online dating consultant. Their more expensive package, about $150, gives you two 200-word essays that can be posted on a dating site.

When you connect with someone you want to get to know a little better, don't spend too much time writing e-mails back and forth; your enthusiasm will start to wane. After some initial correspondence, ask for her phone number and give her a call. Never use your full name in your e-mail address or your profile. You don't want her to track you down should you decide you're not interested. Also, as a precaution, if you don't want to give out your phone number on the first call, you can block it by first dialing *67. Make your first meeting brief. Get together for a cup of coffee or a drink instead of a full meal. And prepare yourself for a lot of cappuccino before finding your next mate.

Once you're ready to begin, you'll find an overwhelming number of dating sites on the Internet. The Internet changes every day—new sites pop up and others close down or merge—but the following chart lists some of the more popular ones for men seeking women, and women seeking men, along with the ages and commitment level of their members, and their intended audience.

NAME:	AmericanSingles.com
AGES:	All
COMMITMENT:	Romance and friendships
AUDIENCE:	All singles

NAME:	Amigos.com
AGES:	All
COMMITMENT:	Friendship to marriage
AUDIENCE:	For Latino singles

NAME:	AnimalPeople.com
AGES:	All
COMMITMENT:	None necessary, other than a desire to be with animal lovers
AUDIENCE:	Don't need to own a pet, but must be single and love animals

NAME:	BlackPeopleMeet.com
AGES:	All
COMMITMENT:	Pen pals to long-term relationships
AUDIENCE:	African American singles

NAME:	BlackPlanet.com
AGES:	All
COMMITMENT:	Dates or professional connections
AUDIENCE:	African American professionals

NAME:	Chemistry.com
AGES:	All
COMMITMENT:	Geared to long-term relationships
AUDIENCE:	All singles; created by the social scientists for Match.com for more specific matches

NAME:	ChristianCafe.com
AGES:	All
COMMITMENT:	Fellowship to marriage
AUDIENCE:	For single Christians of faith; can choose what level of religion you want from a partner

NAME:	ChristianSingles.com
AGES:	Under fifty-five (ChristianSingleSeniors.com for those over fifty-five)
COMMITMENT:	Only for marriage-minded
AUDIENCE:	Christian singles

NAME:	Craigslist.org
AGES:	All
COMMITMENT:	Strictly platonic to romance
AUDIENCE:	Wide range, since the site also lists cars for sale and apartments for rent

NAME:	Dateable.com
AGES:	All
COMMITMENT:	Romance or marriage
AUDIENCE:	Singles looking for romantic lifestyle involving poetry, greeting cards, and other dreamy things

NAME:	Date.com
AGES:	All, but caters to under fifty
COMMITMENT:	Friendship to marriage
AUDIENCE:	All singles

NAME:	DreamMates.com
AGES:	All
COMMITMENT:	Long-term relationships
AUDIENCE:	All singles, drawn by site's membership in Relationship Exchange, a network of online sites that share databases

NAME:	eHarmony.com
AGES:	All
COMMITMENT:	Marriage
AUDIENCE:	All singles willing to fill out extensive questionnaire to find more selective matches

NAME:	Epersonals.com
AGES:	All
COMMITMENT:	Romance or marriage
AUDIENCE:	All singles

NAME:	Friendfinder.com
AGES:	All
COMMITMENT:	In case you're shy about asking for romance, you can find a friend here
AUDIENCE:	All singles

NAME:	Friendster.com
AGES:	All
COMMITMENT:	Companionship rather than marriage
AUDIENCE:	All singles

NAME:	JDate.com
AGES:	All
COMMITMENT:	Romance or marriage
AUDIENCE:	Jewish singles

NAME:	Lavalife.com
AGES:	All, but caters to those in their twenties and thirties
COMMITMENT:	Fun and no commitment
AUDIENCE:	Sexy singles also attracted by this pay-as-you-go site

NAME:	Match.com
AGES:	All
COMMITMENT:	Long-term relationship or marriage
AUDIENCE:	All singles; this granddaddy of all dating sites has the largest database

NAME:	Matchmaker.com
AGES:	All
COMMITMENT:	Marriage
AUDIENCE:	All singles who are comfortable with filling out an in-depth profile

NAME:	MuslimMatch.com
AGES:	All
COMMITMENT:	Friendship to marriage
AUDIENCE:	Muslim singles

NAME:	Nerve.com
AGES:	Caters to those in their twenties and thirties
COMMITMENT:	Dates, not necessarily marriage
AUDIENCE:	Edgy urban singles

NAME:	OkCupid.com
AGES:	All
COMMITMENT:	Marriage
AUDIENCE:	All singles, attracted by this free site created by Harvard and MIT grads and based on mathematical equations to calculate your perfect match

NAME:	MilitarySingles.com
AGES:	All
COMMITMENT:	Long-term relationships
AUDIENCE:	For men and women in uniform, and civilians who want to date them

NAME:	MPwH.net
AGES:	All
COMMITMENT:	Social and support network
AUDIENCE:	For single people with herpes

NAME:	Perfectmatch.com
AGES:	All, but more than half are ages thirty-five to sixty
COMMITMENT:	Lasting relationships
AUDIENCE:	All singles

NAME:	Salon.com
AGES:	All
COMMITMENT:	Look up personals for dates and long-term relationships
AUDIENCE:	All singles

NAME:	PlentyofFish.com
AGES:	All
COMMITMENT:	Dates
AUDIENCE:	Christians to seniors on this site

NAME:	PrimeSingles.net
AGES:	All, but a large database of people over fifty
COMMITMENT:	Romance to marriage
AUDIENCE:	All singles

NAME:	RightStuffDating.com
AGES:	All
COMMITMENT:	Long-term or marriage
AUDIENCE:	Graduates of top colleges

NAME:	SassySeniors.com
AGES:	Over fifty
COMMITMENT:	Friendship to marriage
AUDIENCE:	Single seniors

NAME:	SeniorFriendFinder.com
AGES:	Seniors over fifty
COMMITMENT:	Friends or dates
AUDIENCE:	Single seniors

NAME:	SeniorsCircle.com
AGES:	Over fifty
COMMITMENT:	Companionship or long-term relationship
AUDIENCE:	Single seniors who like the scientific personality profile

NAME:	TallPersonals.com
AGES:	All
COMMITMENT:	Long-term relationships and marriage
AUDIENCE:	For tall men and women

NAME:	True.com
AGES:	All
COMMITMENT:	Long-term relationships
AUDIENCE:	All singles who are drawn to this site, which is endorsed by *Psychology Today* and conducts criminal-background screenings

NAME:	YahooPersonals.com
AGES:	All
COMMITMENT:	Marriage
AUDIENCE:	All singles

Another word about high-tech dating: every year technology evolves and makes dating more and more convenient. You can now use your cell phone to find dates. Since new sites come along all the time, check for these services online.

Dating Services . . . and a Second Mortgage

If you're too busy, too computer-illiterate, or too impatient for fix-ups or online dating, dating services might be your answer. You'll need to have money to burn, though. On average the fees for these services run about $1,000, and there are some that cost upward of $10,000. For this price you are guaranteed a limited number of custom-designed dates. You'll also be required to undergo an extensive interview and reveal a lot of personal information first, such as your salary and phone number. This, by the way, is why baby boomer men, who hate to disclose private details, are so sought-after on dating services, and, consequently, why these services guarantee a deep and rich list of available women. You can locate dating services online or in your phone book. Some of these popular services are listed below.

IT'S JUST LUNCH (WWW.ITSJUSTLUNCH.COM)

FEE:	$1,500 depending on the franchise
SERVICE:	You are set up with roughly a dozen lunch or drink dates. An interview is required but your last name and phone number will not be given out to your prospective dates.

DRIP (WWW.DRIPCAFE.COM)

FEE:	About $15 a month
SERVICE:	You are invited to select an online profile that piques your interest, and they will arrange for you to meet your date in a coffee shop.

GREATEXPECTATIONS (WWW.GE-DATING.COM)

FEE: Between $1,500 and $3,500

SERVICE: You receive videos and personal data to screen and the service then sets up an introductory meeting for you. Check to see if it is available in a city near you, and read the contract carefully before you sign.

EIGHT AT EIGHT (WWW.8AT8.COM)

FEE: An annual fee of about $100 to $500

SERVICE: This is one of several dating services that bring four men and four women together over a gourmet meal. You gather for cocktails, sit down for dinner, pay by separate checks, and then if you are interested in getting to know one of your dinner companions better, the dating service will arrange a date. Search online for "single gourmet" to find a group in a nearby city.

There are several services that offer speed dating events at local restaurants or cafés. You register for an event (usually online) and are then invited to meet about twelve women, typically at a bar or restaurant. You spend a set amount of time chatting with one before the event organizer blows a whistle or gives some other sort of signal, and you move on to the woman at the next table. You repeat this until the event is over. You'll love it—it's like having a remote control for dating.

If you decide you'd like to get to know a particular woman better, the service will inform you if the feeling is mutual and exchange your contact information. The key to success at these events is selling yourself in lightning speed while appearing to be calm, laid-back, and self-assured. Tell her what you do for a living, the ages of your kids, and, if there is time, what you like to do in your spare time. Then give her a chance to do the same.

Speed dating events typically cost about $35 to $50 and can be found online. Here are some of the larger companies.

CUPID.COM/PREDATING	Spend six minutes talking with up to twelve women.
FASTLIFE.COM	Eight minutes with ten single women in a cocktail party setting, currently available in several major cities.
HURRYDATE.COM	Sets up its events by age range, religion, race, or sexual preference. After three minutes with a prospective date, you head to the next possibility.
SPEEDDATING.COM	A seven-minute round-robin dating event for Jewish singles.
8MINUTEDATING.COM	Eight minutes to meet the person with whom you could end up spending the rest of your life.

If you have little time to search for dates and have disposable income, you could consider hiring a matchmaker, who acts as a dating counselor. He or she will not only find you the perfect match but arrange the introduction as well. You can find these companies online by plugging "matchmakers" into a search engine. For the privacy, discretion, and custom dates that they guarantee, you can pay well over $10,000 or even $25,000.

How's Internet dating sounding now?

First Date: Talk Is Cheap, but You Aren't

Since a first date often follows a casual get-together over coffee or a drink or a lengthy phone conversation, it should provide an opportunity for you both to learn a lot more about each other. Forget the movies. Sitting shoulder to shoulder silently for two and half hours kills time but does nothing to further a relationship. Instead, plan a lunch or a dinner in a restaurant that is quiet enough for you to hear each other speak, and tasteful enough that you won't be rushed through your meal. Skip self-serve places such as coffeehouses or sandwich shops. They are great for a first meeting but not for a first date.

If you want to try something a little more novel than a meal, invite her to a museum, a park, or a ball game, either professional or college. You can also pick an activity in which you shine, especially if you think it will ease your nerves. Maybe when you were in high school you bowled, played ice hockey, or performed in the school orchestra. Show off your talents, but don't be obnoxious about it. She'll get a little closer to your world, which she will find very appealing.

Both of you will be curious to know why the other is divorced, how a spouse died, why he or she never married. It's natural to be curious about this, so ask. Let her give you a brief response and then offer one in return: "My wife and I hadn't communicated in ten years" or "My wife went through a midlife crisis and sought a different life. It happens. We've both moved on." End of story. To be continued...when you and she have dated a lot more. It's unappealing for either of you to bad-mouth an ex-spouse or, like the guy I dated, praise one. The objective is for you to get to know this new woman, not to dwell on the past.

Warren believes that "sometimes it's easy to talk about past relationships, since they are often the fodder for current relationships." While it may be easy to talk about something so familiar, you don't want to do this on a first date. And if she does, it probably means she's not over her ex or she's stuck in the past. Eat quickly and suddenly remember you promised to take your daughter to the mall.

What you should talk about on a first date is your kids and hers, if she has any. Make sure you have a few pictures in your wallet. Show her your children and tell her (modestly) about their strengths. Let her know whether they live with you or their mother and how much time you spend with them. Be honest without revealing anything that might scare her off. (She doesn't need to know your son collects lizards or your daughter is addicted to body piercings.) Then, without missing a beat, ask about her kids. This is critical. If you show an interest in a woman's kids, it sends a signal to her that you are relationship material.

Chances are your first date will end with a check. She may make a good salary, possibly even more than you, and she probably believes in equal relationships. But the truth is, on a first date most women want to be treated. Even if we offer to pick up the check or share the cost, we still want you to override our offer and pay the bill. You'll score some brownie points too. If you continue to date a person, treating may automatically become more fifty-fifty.

However, some women will be uncomfortable having you pay but may be equally uncomfortable picking up the check or splitting it. These women should reciprocate by inviting you to dinner at their home, buying tickets to a show, or finding some way to treat you. You deserve to be appreciated for your generosity.

Nearly all the men I interviewed agreed they would pick up the check on a first date. Drew says he'll always pick it up "even if it was the worst date in the world." However, David says that although he is chivalrous, if she has invited him to a meal, he expects her to pay. I agree with this, too. You can still offer, but you are not obligated if she invited you.

Once you've taken care of the check and your first date draws to a close, you're faced with another critical step—do you kiss her goodnight? It seems trivial to be talking about kissing on the first date when we've become a culture no longer shocked by one-night stands. But the subject of kissing will more than likely cross your mind as you walk her to her door or car. Conrad says he never knows what he's supposed to do, so he waits until the fourth or fifth date to kiss a woman. You really don't have to wait that long. If you've met casually for a light meal, then a handshake or, if there is some warmth and chemistry, a hug or kiss on the cheek will suffice. But after two or three *official* dates, if you haven't kissed her goodnight yet, she's going to be wondering.

Robert says he hugs good-bye on the first couple of dates but waits until the third or fourth before he asks, "Can I kiss you?" Again, Robert worries a little about his image as a teacher in his small town, where everyone knows who he is. Being exceedingly well mannered is a smart decision for him. Alan, too, says that when he met that woman from JDate in person, she made it pretty clear their first date would be very casual. "We met for coffee and we each paid our way. We shook hands when we said good-bye. She said she was shocked by how many guys tried to hug and kiss her after an initial meeting. When I did hug her for the first time I actually asked permission. It wasn't that I was being old-fashioned; I just thought it was the appropriate thing to do."

A lot of the men I talked to say they'll shake hands when in doubt. On an introductory meeting that is fine, but after that, it feels a little weird. Give her a hug. Drew says he purposely uses a handshake if he doesn't want to see them again; otherwise they get a good-bye kiss on the cheek. If you are unsure how a woman will react, then ask permission as Robert and Alan did. No woman will be annoyed at that. If she's the one to initiate the kissing, the ball's in your court. It's your decision to embrace it or to carefully back away. If you see it coming and want to head her off at the pass, be proactive and kiss her on the cheek.

What if you never want to see her again? Do you ask for her number at the end of the date just to be courteous and eliminate any awkwardness? No. Just tell her it was nice meeting her and don't commit to any future plans. Every woman would rather know how you feel from the get-go than be let down later. No matter what you think of her, be kind. If she didn't get the hint and calls or e-mails you, then be more direct. Tell her, "I did enjoy meeting you, but at this point, I don't think the chemistry is there. I don't want to waste your time." If she persists despite your gentle rejection, just tell her, "It is not going to work out. Good-bye."

The reason you remain as polite as possible (other than the fact that it's the right thing to do) is that you are well aware that the shoe could be on the other foot. You have just mustered up all your shaky confidence to ask out a woman. You like her, but when you phone her for a second date, she may not return your call. With caller ID, it's rare today for any woman not to know who is on the other end of the line. It's okay to try twice, possibly once by phone and once by e-mail. But after that, take her hint and let it go. The rejection is a reflection on her, not on you. She's looking for someone a little different from you—not better, just a better match.

Woman, the Aggressor

The possibility of being with another woman felt so remote to Jason that when his late wife's close friend announced she was going to take care of him, he was clueless as to her actual intentions. She'd make dinner for both of their families every Sunday and they'd talk on the phone for hours. She'd also confide in him about her dates. One evening after dinner, Jason accidentally brushed her shoulder, and that tiny physical contact set her off on a stream of confession. "I love you," she said. "You're the one for me. We are a perfect match." Jason says he should have seen it coming. "Friends would say, 'Why don't you take her out?' I'd say, 'No. I don't want to be another notch on her bedpost.'" So Jason told her he appreciated her feelings but just wasn't yet in a position to understand his own. Then several weeks later she needed an escort to a black-tie affair. Jason reluctantly agreed to go. The combination of drink, dance, and romance led to kissing. The next thing he knew, they were entangled in her sheets . . . and then in an intense and serious relationship.

Jason's situation is by no means unique. Women can be just as aggressive as men—unabashedly so. Dwight got a call from a neighbor right after his wife died. "She phoned me out of the blue. She said, 'I heard about your wife. I saw the obituary. How would you like to go out?'" I know a brazen woman who one day appeared unannounced in the office of a newly divorced dentist and told the receptionist she was single and would like to meet him. He hid in his office the rest of the day.

You may also find that women are more aggressive when it comes to sex than you remember the last time you dated. Okay, wipe the smile off your face and listen up. Don't mistake a woman who is great in bed for one who will sleep with anyone from her boss to her plumber. There's a reason women TiVo *Desperate Housewives.*

Even a seemingly shy, timid woman might shock you when it comes to the physical side of a relationship. Remember that sweet lady David met in church? When he finally called her back, she invited him over to bake cookies. It doesn't get more June Cleaver than that. As soon as the temperature rose for the cookies, so did hers. "She threw herself at me. I wasn't ready for that," he says.

I'm telling you about this side of women because as new as it is for you, it's new for some of them, too. While you were in a long monogamous marriage that perhaps had become less physical, so were many of them. Remember, women peak sexually much later than men, so the sexual attitudes of the women you're meeting now may seem very different from what you remember when you and your wife dated. And most women today are much more comfortable with their sexuality than they were twenty years ago. Enjoy this liberating development, but remember that physical attraction isn't necessarily love.

Way Too Much Information

As soon as you start dating, you will probably be anxious to talk to someone for advice. As I've mentioned, it's imperative to tell your kids you are dating, but it is inappropriate to involve them in the entire process, as tempting as that may be. You come home from a wonderful date to be greeted by your daughter. "How was it?" she asks. You don't want to sound evasive by merely responding, "Great." Going into more detail is fine as long as you're sharing basic information that is in no way intimate. "Man, she was so hot" or "Her ex-husband cheated on her" is not an appropriate response. These are adult details better left said—if they must be said at all—to a friend. The majority of dads recognize this distinction and make a point of confiding only in other adults. In fact, my survey reveals that 68 percent of single dads confide in friends, family, coworkers, a therapist, or other adults about their dates. Eighteen percent say they confide in their kids, and 17 percent say they don't feel comfortable discussing their dates with anybody. Interestingly, the dads who have kids old enough to empathize with dating—teenagers—rarely confide in them.

Warren chooses to confide in his friends. He says that even though guys usually tend to be less talkative about personal matters, he has found the opposite to be the case with his buddies. "Oddly, a lot of them are either divorced, on their way to getting divorced, or in marriages they can't stand, so there is plenty to talk about," he admits. "Guys supposedly don't like to talk about it, but believe me, they talk. Sex is the first thing they talk about. Of course, we are no more honest than when we were eighteen. I'd say the 20 percent embellishment factor is still in play. By the time they are in their late forties everything is the 'most amazing thing.' But you play along with it because those are the rules."

This is precisely the reason Conrad doesn't talk to his guy friends. Not only doesn't he want their input, but now that he's fifty-four, he's no longer interested in the type of locker-room banter that he and his friends engaged in when they were dating in their twenties. He makes a good point. Any relationship you have now should be treated with respect. This woman could become your next wife and your kids' stepmom. Drew also feels this way and consequently confides only in his therapist. He feels that most of his friends don't fully comprehend his situation. As Drew says, "It's a self-awareness journey, and there are only so many people you want to take on your journey."

So what *is* suitable to discuss with your kids? Most children like being privy to certain facts, but you'll quickly get the wave of the hand signaling "that's too much information" if you start revealing personal details. You can, and should, tell them whom you are dating—her name, her age, whether she has kids, what she does for a living, and where you went on a date. Keep to yourself that you barely watched any of the movie, the food was cold by the time you got to it, and her dog is overprotective of her. No kid, not even your teenager, wants to know all this. If you want to involve your kids on a level they can relate to, then ask for fashion tips or for a restaurant recommendation. They'll be flattered that you value their choices. Sarah says her dad will always seek her opinion on his clothing, and she has no qualms telling him the truth. In fact, she likes that he asks for her advice.

With older children, you may find yourself trading stories about dating. Ben does this, carefully. Even when his son asks personal questions, Ben reveals very little about his relationships. Intimate details are inappropriate, but if you start to have feelings for a woman, you should let your kids know. Daniel had no idea his father was in love with a woman until they broke up: "I hadn't seen him heartbroken like that since my mom died." When fourteen-year-old Tom's father began dating his late wife's friend, he confided in his son that he thought he was falling for her. Tom says, "I told him just do what your heart and brain tell you, and if you're wrong, you'll learn a lesson. You won't learn a lesson if it's too easy."

Wow, who are the adults here?

Dating has changed a lot since the first time you drove up to a girl's house in your 1970 Camaro and met her father at the door. But then, so have you. You're closer to the father who opened the door than the kid in the Camaro. Fortunately, the opportunities to meet someone are greater today than they were just a decade ago. You can find dates in all sorts of ways, from fix-ups to the Internet. Get out there and enjoy yourself, but always be mindful of your kids.

3

The Bermuda Triangle: Your Kids, Your Date, Your Ex

You probably recognize this scenario.

You are sprucing up for a date, whistling to yourself, dabbing on the cologne, and sliding the belt buckle over a notch because your predawn workouts have begun to pay off. A quick glance at your watch confirms you have just enough time to stop for gas. You sprint down the stairs, unleashing a barely containable grin. But as your foot grazes the bottom step, you hit a snag: your thirteen-year-old.

"Dad, I need a ride to Jamie's house."

"Why didn't you say something earlier? I don't have time now."

"Because she just called."

"I can't. I'm going to be late."

"What, you get to go out and have a good time and I have to stay home by myself?"

Wouldn't it be nice if you could say, "You bet. See you later"? But you're a parent; worse, you're a single parent, and you hate to disappoint your children, who have dealt with enough distress in their short lives. So you reluctantly tell your date you're going to be late because you have to take your daughter someplace first.

Score: child, one; father, zero.

As a single dad, you're attuned to your kids' requests and usually are happy to oblige. But when you begin dating, their demands—even when reasonable—are on a direct collision course with your social life. Remember, you're the driver here. You can't allow any child, whether it's yours or hers, to orchestrate the relationship between two adults. At the same time, you can't ever let a woman come between you and your kids. So how do you balance these competing needs? It's a little like a game of tug-of-war. Only in this version, you're not rooting for either side—you're just trying to maintain an equilibrium.

And once you think you've found that delicate balance, a third personality enters the fray: your former wife. If she isn't dating anyone, your children feel sorry for her. If she is, your eager-to-please kids are dealing with another man, possibly a stepdad, and maybe even an extended family. Even if you are widowed, the memory of your late wife directly impacts your relationship with a new woman, as well as your kids' feelings about her. In either situation, you'll find that in order to date well, you have to parent well, which means first understanding what your children are facing.

Divided Loyalties

It was an icy February night, just two days before Valentine's Day, and an enthusiastic Tracey arrived at the high school gym for her championship basketball game. As she bent over to tie her sneakers, the coach entered the locker room and announced, "We have a special surprise tonight. Each of you will hand a rose to your mom before the game starts." Both Tracey's mom and stepmother were sitting in the bleachers.

"I didn't know what to do," Tracey says. "Of course I would go to my mother first. I felt bad going to my stepmother at all, yet I didn't want to leave her out. It was just one of those situations in which I felt awkward and wondered to myself, 'Why can't I just have *a* mom?'" In the end, Tracey asked her coach for two roses and handed one to each woman.

All kids who are products of divorce can relate to Tracey's predicament at some level. Yet as parents, we sometimes fail to appreciate our children's Solomonic dilemma. Even during the regular basketball season, Tracey still had to pick which parent to approach first at the end of a game. To this day, she and her brothers find holidays and birthday parties particularly stressful as they diplomatically try to split their time between Mom and Dad.

Neither my first husband, Charlie, nor I had divorced parents, yet when we began dating we wanted to please both sets so badly that we ate two Thanksgiving dinners, one at noon at his parents' house and one at 6:00 P.M. at mine. I couldn't look at a sweet potato pie until Easter. Once married, we invited both families to our home for Thanksgiving. Our solution was simple because our parents were still married. In divorced families, children rarely have the opportunity to celebrate holidays with both parents together. And as each parent finds a new significant other with his or her own relatives to include, the family tree starts to dwarf the Christmas spruce at Rockefeller Center.

"On Thanksgiving and other holidays we split the day," Tracey says. "We usually wake up early at my mom's, then go to my dad's for a few hours. Later we come back to my mom's for a little while and then go back to my dad's. At the end of the night, we go back to my mother's to sleep. Now that I have a boyfriend, I don't get to spend time with his family. Holidays are never relaxing. If we're at my mom's, Dad calls and wants to know when we're coming over. If we're at Dad's, Mom calls and asks when we're coming back. They always use the 'this may be your grandmother's last Christmas' line."

The only reason we put our kids through this dizzying game of holiday ping-pong is because we want to be with them. But try to understand that your kids' family life spun out of control when you divorced. Give them back some of that control and ask them what they'd like to do. Would it be easier to alternate the holidays every year? Or celebrate Thanksgiving with one parent Wednesday night and the other Thursday? Christmas Eve with one and Christmas day with the other? If it means you will be alone on the holiday itself, make plans to be with friends. Don't make your kids feel guilty because they are with Mom and her boyfriend and you are home alone cozying up to a Hungry-Man dinner.

It's not just the infrequent holidays that put a strain on the kids—it's the day-to-day living arrangements. Like so many families, Justin's parents share custody. Four mornings a week Justin and his siblings awake at dawn, climb into their mother's car, and drive twenty miles to their father's house to meet their school bus. The arrangement works for both parents, who get to live in their own homes, but the kids are exhausted from trying to please everyone.

Remember, kids of single parents feel somewhat responsible for their mother's and father's happiness. If they were oblivious to their parents' moods before, now they pick up on your every word, action, or frown. What a burden that is on your kids. Be cognizant of this while you are dating and let it guide you in how you communicate with them. Look for signs of stress, such as changes in sleeping and eating habits or difficulties in school and with friends, and talk to them about their anxiety. When you do, Dr. Halpern suggests you make direct statements rather than ask questions: *I know you are angry and upset, and that's normal. I will not be angry at you if you are having difficulty adjusting to your new life and to my dating. I understand.* Give them permission to have these feelings.

Then, after you remind them that you love them more than anything in the world, you could say: *In time, as you*

get older, you'll see how life sometimes throws us challenges.
When they happen to us as children, we become very smart and
capable adults. I know it's tough learning life lessons so young. If
they remain unresponsive, bring them to a therapist or a
school counselor or ask your child's teacher or pediatrician
to recommend someone. It's not unusual for children to resist outside help at first, but they usually end up benefiting
from it. With more than thirty-two million single-parent
households in this country, your child is far from the only
one in his or her class going through a family trauma.

If, in your case, you had an affair or left your family, you
may find that your children are resentful, distrusting of
you, and acting out. After all, you broke the family's un-
written rules, so why can't they? In order for you to once
again hold moral authority, you have to admit your mistakes. Tell your children you are so sorry for the pain
you've caused them and that you will live with your regrets for the rest of your life. While some kids will challenge your authority in a situation such as this, others may
direct their ire against the other parent. According to Dr.
Halpern, some children want so badly to appease the parent who left that they make excuses for him or her. "It's
based on a fear of abandonment," he says. "They actually
treat the parent who left better. The parent who remains
bears the brunt of the child's anger, but that's because that
child feels greater intimacy and trust with that parent."

Your children need to view you as the adult in charge
whose job it is to protect and provide a secure environment. Sometimes that means instituting rules that seem
unfair, especially since you may not follow them yourself.

"As a father, you love them enough to say, 'I'm the father. You're the child. I know better how to protect you than you do,'" says Dr. Halpern.

We also burden our kids unfairly when we confide in them about our former spouse, sometimes to complain, other times to extract information. Discrediting your ex-wife in front of your kids will weigh heavily on them, sometimes leaving an impression they will be unable to shake. While it may affect their view of her, more than likely it will negatively affect their opinion of you as someone they can trust. She is their mother, and since your goal is to raise emotionally healthy children, they should never hear you say a bad word about her or—bite your tongue— her latest boyfriend. If your ex-wife is a poor mother, your kids will figure that out on their own and will need even more support from you.

Your kids also hate to be placed in the middle when you confide in them about your life and then demand they keep it a secret from their mother. You're not intending to be malicious, but you simply don't want your ex-wife to be privy to the details of your new life. Think about it, though—is it really a big deal if she finds out you bought that fifty-inch plasma television you always wanted? Probably not. Maybe you don't want to upset her with the more significant news that you have a girlfriend. Regardless of the scope of the "secret," you have unintentionally placed your kids in an untenable position. They never want to hide information from their mother on your behalf. Tracey echoes the sentiment of most children when she says that anything you tell your kids should be made available to their mother if she should ask. Otherwise, don't tell them. "I do remember when my mom's boyfriend started coming and staying for the weekend," she says. "I don't know why, but initially my mom didn't want my father to know about him. So I was told not to say anything. This happened a lot. 'Don't tell your mom.' 'Don't tell your dad.' I hated lying. I got really good at avoiding the question."

Dr. Halpern says to instruct your children to say to each parent, " 'I do not need or want to talk about it. If you want, call Dad or Mom and ask them directly.' Don't force them to lie to their mother. It's disrespectful to her and it undermines her image in your child's eyes. Forcing your kids into this position is very destructive and painful and borders on emotional abuse."

David says when his children return from a visit with their mother, he doesn't ask about her, despite the temptation. "I don't ask. I don't want to know," he says. Then, hesitating, he admits: "Well, I do and I don't. Truthfully, I want to know that she's miserable, but I don't like that in myself." It's normal to feel this way; just don't share these feelings with your kids.

Mike hates that his dad forces him to lie to his mother. When his dad admitted to having a two-year relationship with a much younger woman, he instructed his son not to tell his mom. "It was an awful position for me to be put in. It was really difficult knowing that this had to be our little secret. I felt like I was betraying my mother." When Mike's mom finally learned that his father was dating, she was furious and hurt that her kids had kept it from her.

Tracey feels that being asked to keep the secrets of each parent is a betrayal of the other "whether you lie or tell the truth and reveal something the other one doesn't want to know." Her advice to parents: "Be honest with everybody, your kids and your ex. As a kid, the two people you love most in the world are your parents, and when they don't love each other and hate each other sometimes, it hurts." Sharing confidential information about your love life only adds to the pain.

You may be a sensitive and considerate father who works very hard at not compromising his children, but if your ex-spouse doesn't date, your kids may still be forced to split loyalties. To them, their mom can appear to be lonely and sad. This is not your fault, and there is little you can do about it short of finding a guy to fix her up with. Your kids may even feel responsible for her happiness and companionship if she chooses to remain unattached and uses her loneliness in a manipulative way. Fortunately, most children are keenly observant, and ultimately—especially as they mature—will see through this type of behavior.

Mike is conflicted because his mother doesn't date. He has tried to get to know his father's girlfriend, who he says is very nice, but the fact that his mother isn't seeing someone makes any connection he has with this woman feel like a betrayal of his mom. Even though his mother insists she accepts her ex-husband's dating, the contrast of her being alone and Dad having a partner is not lost on Mike. "If my mom were in a serious relationship, that would make a difference. I would feel a little less awkward about it," he says.

Tracey, too, says her relationship with both her parents is less strained now that her mother has become engaged. Until this time, Tracey has felt a need to protect her mom since it was her dad who left. And even though both parents tried to keep their personal difficulties from the kids, inevitably Tracey and her siblings worried about their mother being alone.

Nick says his relationship with his children has suffered because he initiated the divorce and found someone very quickly, while his wife decided not to date. Consequently, his children feel sorry for their mom. In Alan's case, his ex-wife has chosen to delay marrying her longtime boyfriend until their youngest child turns eighteen. He says, "She claims she could never shrink her love for her kids. It's a shot back at me because I didn't wait to remarry."

As you know by now, you can't control the thoughts or actions of anyone but you. If your ex-spouse doesn't date, you need to say to your kids: "It's Mom's choice. It's important that she be happy regardless of whether she chooses to date. I'm so sorry that you are hurt by this."

Of course, if you're the unattached parent, your children will pity you. Drew admits that his son is worried that he doesn't have a girlfriend: "He feels bad that Daddy doesn't have anybody and Mommy does. I tell him, 'This is my choice right now.' "

In situations of divorce, the divided loyalties faced by the children are usually fairly obvious. But what happens in the case of a parent who has died? These kids often cannot comprehend Dad's need to be with another woman, and assume he has forgotten about Mom. Needless to say, this is far from the truth, but if other adults have difficulty accepting a widower dating, imagine how the kids must feel.

Christine's father constantly lamented over his deceased wife, so when he eventually became engaged to another woman, his daughter was happy for him and didn't see it as an abandonment of her mom. She also felt grateful that her dad wouldn't be alone when she left for college. Nancy, who is only in middle school, believes her dad is forsaking her mom by dating other women. "I don't want my dad to forget about her. It seems like he is trying to," she says. You can help your kids see that this just isn't the case. Continue to talk about their mom, both in front of them and eventually in front of them and your new girl-friend. At least until you are engaged or remarried, keep pictures on display of the kids with you and their mom. Your children will grieve for the loss of that parent for a very long time, but as they mature and enter adult relation-ships they will understand your need and desire for new companionship.

Who's Running the Show?

Remember when you and your children's mom would ar-rive home from a dinner party at 2:00 A.M.? The babysitter had put the kids to bed by 10:00 P.M., as you instructed. No one, not even your kids, questioned your rules. After all, you and their mom were the adults in the household. Now that you date as a single father, you notice something has changed. You try to set rules for your kids, but they seem to think they can set them for you. Conrad had given his daughter an 11:00 P.M. curfew when she started high school. This went unchallenged until he began dating. "It's not fair," she insisted. "If I have to be home by eleven, then so do you."

Just because your children now have a single father, the need for household rules has not changed. If earlier you insisted upon curfews or limited television time until their grades improved, there is no reason to change your thinking now. And as far as the rules governing your new social life go, so long as you remain a responsible parent, tell your kids that the privilege of being an adult is that those decisions are left up to you. Remain cognizant, though, that these observant little sponges see and internalize everything you do and may throw your indiscretions right back at you when the time is ripe; that is, when it benefits them. While you don't need to have a curfew for yourself, you do need to tell your children what time you will be home, and you need to adhere to that time. It's not fair to them, and it's irresponsible of you, if you promise to be home at 1:00 A.M. and instead roll in with the morning newspaper.

The irony is that even if your children complain about the rules you set for them, they don't actually want to push you around. Dr. Halpern says that when parents surrender too much power, kids can feel unprotected. "The more you give in, the more they lose respect for you," he says. "You are also creating anxiety in them. Limitations, consequences, and consistent follow-through provide your kids with a sense of security."

He says that a single dad can also be overly accommodating out of fear of permanently alienating his children, or because he is easily manipulated by guilt. "Men who are pretty healthy emotionally try to keep a balance. They want to be attentive and sensitive to a new person they are dating but not desert their kids. They are the ones who realize their kids have been through enough. They've already lost one parent through divorce or death, and now all of a sudden Dad is out several nights a week."

Sometimes the boundaries you set for your children are exacerbated by a mother who, deliberately or not, contradicts your efforts. If your kids can control their mother, then Dad becomes the bad guy. Alan says his daughter has learned to control her mother. "My daughter is on her fifth therapist. She and my ex keep firing them. She's having boundary issues and has learned to manipulate her mother. I don't let her do it to me. She always needs the extras— everyone else will be fine with water, but she'll have to have a milk shake."

Dr. Halpern says that Alan is correct in not giving in to his daughter's demands. He should explain to her that he expects the same behavior from all his kids. She doesn't need special treatment. "When most kids get older they look back and are thankful to the parent who set boundaries for them," adds Dr. Halpern.

Some kids are so needy for your attention they just can't

help being manipulative. They might express it by claiming to be sick as you're leaving to go out, or by calling your cell phone repeatedly when you're in a restaurant with a date. First try to understand the motivation behind this behavior. Is your child scared to be alone? Is there a reason he doesn't trust this woman? Maybe she's affectionate to you but cold to him. Is he afraid you'll lose interest in him? Tell your child: "I know it's a little weird for you to see Daddy with some woman you barely know. Honestly, it's a little weird for me, too. But I know that eventually we both will become more comfortable with it. In the meantime, you have to give me some time alone with this woman so I can figure out if I even like her well enough and if she'll fit in with our family." And then—since you can't reinforce this enough—tell your child that no woman will ever come between the two of you.

Gary admits that he feels so bad for his three daughters that he intentionally spoils them. His eldest daughter, who is thirteen and has given him the most difficult time about his social life, owns sixteen pairs of designer jeans. "I spend money like you wouldn't believe," he says. "I spoil all of them, and it's kind of causing a problem. My eldest wants to shop at Neiman Marcus. I hate to deprive them. They've been deprived enough."

Halpern says you should acknowledge the painful effect that their parents' divorce or their mother's death had on their lives, but then explain that it doesn't mean they can have everything they want. He says to tell them, "You're right, it *is* tough. Things have happened to our family and we all have to make some adjustments. I'm sorry that you can't always have what you wish. But money is an issue, and we all have to chip in and make compromises." Involve the kids in finding a solution as well. Have them prioritize what really matters to them. Is it the jeans, or the sneakers, or a trip over Christmas vacation? By empowering them to choose, you are showing your kids that you are trying very hard to provide them with what they want, and consequently they will value their selection.

I understand what drives us as single parents to give our kids everything we possibly can. We want to compensate for the loss they neither requested nor caused. We know it's not fair that their childhood veered off course, so we overcompensate. We are all guilty of this sometimes. I remember when my son made a travel soccer team. A week later, another coach called to tell me he had made a travel hockey team. My mother said, "You're a single mom. Your son will have to choose one team." I remember saying to her, "Why should he be denied what he has rightfully earned just because I'm a single parent? He's already suffered an unfair loss in his life." So, like a lot of us, I burned the candle at both ends—physically and financially—so my son could be like all the other boys in the neighborhood.

As single parents, we don't just indulge our kids by giving them material goods or overextending ourselves to accommodate their lives. Too many of us don't demand that they help out at home. We feel guilty asking them to do chores even though we need their help now more than ever. If you share custody with their mother, you may want to create a fun home for them so they keep coming back to see you. In the meantime, not only do you suffer as a single parent, but you have cheated your kids out of an opportunity to learn how to take care of themselves. If your life is hectic, do you really think it is okay for your son to be sitting on the sofa playing video games? Feeling like part of a team, helping out, and pitching in with his share of the chores is not punishment. In fact, it is an affirmation that you are a family. When your kids stay with you, they are not guests but fully involved members of the clan. If you have established a home environment in which your children have responsibility, they will be better adjusted to the concept of cooperation and sharing if, at some point, you blend them with another family.

After devoting years to raising their kids, some dads ultimately stop deferring to them and get on with their lives. Dwight, who waited until his kids were in high school to date, says his youngest daughter has always been less accepting of his social life. He says, "She expects to be the sole focus of my attention, even to this day. She just told her older sister that because I moved out of the house she grew up in, she considers herself homeless. She's twenty-four!"

David, too, had put off having a social life for years after his wife left him. He was the primary caregiver and concentrated his energies on raising his kids. Now that he has started dating, he has asked all of his kids to go to counseling. "My daughter is having the most difficulty with my dating. So she's going to therapy even if she just sits there for an hour. I know it will help."

Even though at times you won't please anyone—your kids or your ex or your girlfriend—try to trust your instincts. Just because you are a single father doesn't mean you should raise your kids any differently from when you were married to their mom. They're still your kids, and you are still their dad.

Daddy's Little Girl

Gary pulled up to the supermarket at 10:00 P.M. on a mission. First he grabbed a huge bag of dog food, and then he headed to the feminine products aisle. He peered in all directions and when the coast was clear, he tossed box after box of tampons into his cart with little regard to the brand or size or style. Then, before heading to the cashier, he covered up the whole lot in his cart—an astonishing $70 worth—with the bag of dog food.

"I bought a variety of brands so I wouldn't have to go back for a long time. Although her aunt had explained the basics, my daughter, who's only eleven, asked me to buy her tampons, and I was uncomfortable. So I went late at night, and wandered around the grocery store until I finally ended up in front of the right shelves."

After he stuffed the loot into his car and hurried home to his daughter, he found himself in an even more awkward situation as he tried to help her from the other side of the bathroom door.

"Dad, I'm not getting it right."

"Look at the carton," Gary instructed. "Look at the pictures on the box."

"Dad, it's not working."

So Gary got out a medical book and showed her some helpful illustrations. And then she returned to the privacy of the bathroom. "I talked through the door and she did it. I told her it was uncomfortable for me as well as for her. But in a strange way it was a bonding moment."

This is a common but uncomfortable circumstance for single dads. In all likelihood, if the child's mother is available, she will assume the role of helping her daughter through this sudden arrival of puberty. But many single dads have no choice other than to step up to the plate and, like Gary, go through the embarrassment of buying feminine products for their daughters. You know that it should be no big deal, but it still can feel like contraband in your shopping cart.

David says his daughter has no compunction about asking him to get the ones "in the blue box, unscented, with wings," and it no longer bothers him. "They could even get me up there and yell 'Price check!' and I would be okay," he says. "I'm just being a dad for my daughter."

If you have a daughter, you've probably already discovered that it can be somewhat embarrassing to discuss the facts of life with her. Mothers have the same level of discomfort with their sons. When the time came, I enlisted the thirty-year-old son of a close family friend to take Noah out to lunch and discuss sex. I knew my son, who was twelve, would be more comfortable talking to another male about intimate subjects rather than his mom. Frankly, I also had no clue as to what he already knew.

If it's easier for both of you to involve a woman, then get help from an aunt, the mother of a school friend, a teacher, or a female doctor. Seth says he and his kids were away on vacation when his daughter got her first period. Fortunately, his daughter's girlfriend had traveled with them. The girlfriend kept asking a curious and confused Seth to drive her to the drugstore. When they returned home from their vacation, the girlfriend's mother informed Seth that his daughter had gotten her period and was embarrassed to talk to him about it. Although she's become a little more relaxed discussing such personal things with her dad, Seth says she still prefers to talk to a female family friend. "Even when she asks me about makeup or other things, I have her call a family friend who can give her the skinny."

These developmental issues aside, your daughter adores you more than you know. In fact, the bond between a father and daughter is so unique that sometimes the presence of another woman other than Mom is viewed as an intrusion. Having been that intruder, I know it is very difficult to compete with Daddy's Little Girl. Many fathers are so awestruck, even a bit intimidated, by a daughter, they are unaware they've been wrapped around her little finger. As Dr. Halpern says, parents are generally a little stricter with the child of their same gender. It's the "been there, done that" scenario. But our child of the opposite gender is an enigma to us. I remember when my son grew taller than me, his voice began to deepen, and his feet outgrew his sneakers every three weeks—I was admittedly in awe. Boys did that?

While you are enamored by your daughter—as many dads are—be careful not to shut out your girlfriend. You might think it's adorable that your teenage daughter always plops down next to you on the sofa when your date gets up to use the bathroom, but the two women have a language all their own. Trust me, you're a guy, you can't hear it. It's like a whistle audible only to dogs. Each woman is being territorial, and you are the territory.

Dr. Halpern says this type of behavior is fairly typical because girls are generally possessive of their father's attention and feel threatened by another woman. They fear that Dad will be so distracted by her that he'll forget about them. It's your job to make sure your daughter knows that will never happen, but now that you are dating it's reasonable to expect her support—or at least her acquiescence. Your other job is to assure your girlfriend that you will not be sidetracked by your daughter's attempts to steal your attention.

David and Alan have both found that their daughters are less accepting of their girlfriends than are their sons. David's daughter often uses her sadness over her parents' divorce as an attention-getting device. Alan says that while his sons approve of his dating, his daughter is dead set against it. "Her brothers don't understand her reaction."

Dr. Halpern says, "Sensitive boys have the same objections as the girls. The rough-and-tumble boys may feel it too, but they don't voice it. Instead, they might act out more. Sometimes it's shown as defiance toward the new girlfriend: 'This woman can't tell me what to do. She's not my mother. I don't have to listen to her. I don't have to like her.'"

Regardless of whether your daughter likes your girlfriend, you may find her assuming another role: that of Mom as Authority Figure. Seth finds this to be the case with his teenage daughter. "In some respects my daughter has taken on that job. She now thinks it's her place to nag me about the same things my wife used to nag me about. I tell her, 'You're the child here. Even if I act like the child, you *are* still the child.'" Seth bought a convertible after his wife passed away (not an unusual splurge for a newly single dad) and didn't tell his children. When his daughter came home from school and saw the shiny new car in the garage, she was incensed. "Dad, you can't spend money like that. We don't need this." Seth told her, "It's Dad's toy. Leave me alone." In the absence of her mother, his daughter feels she has two roles to fill.

Alan had a similar experience. When he took his kids and his girlfriend to Disney World over Thanksgiving, his fifteen-year-old daughter chided him for drinking a glass of wine. "I had to call her on it. She was acting like my mother, and it was inappropriate."

There are a couple of reasons a daughter thinks she needs to parent her dad. One is a sense of loyalty to her mom, who would most assuredly disapprove of Dad's "irresponsible" behavior, and the other is the assumption that Dad can't take care of himself. Since we all act a little like carefree teenagers when we begin dating, we open ourselves up to this perception. Calmly and authoritatively, let your daughter know that you are well aware of how much money you have to spend without blowing the family budget or how much wine you can drink without becoming intoxicated, and while you appreciate her concern, you are the parent and she is the child. And these roles will remain unchanged even when you are ninety-five and in a nursing home.

All you can do is hope she'll come by for a visit and give you a ride in her convertible.

What Do They *Really* Think of Her?

As single parents nothing would make us happier than for our children to love the person with whom we fall in love. One big happy family. The Brady Bunch (without Alice). But sometimes our kids don't particularly like the person we're dating, or at best feel ambivalent and just can't understand Dad's attraction. Should you allow your kids' opinions to determine how you ultimately feel about a woman? Typically not, but they should be a factor. And there will be times when their intuition is worth heeding.

Not only does it take courage for you to ask your children what they think about a woman you're dating, it takes courage for them to give you an honest answer. First try to distinguish between their genuine dislike and discomfort, and then have the following conversation.

"I've been dating Betsy for two months now. Do you think you're getting to know her any better?"

"A little."

"I think she would like to spend more time with us as a family."

"Whatever. I don't care."

"I do care. Because I love you and your sister and I like her very much, I would like all of us to get to know her better."

"Uh-huh."

"Is there anything you want me to know?"

"I hate that she always talks about her kids and shows no interest in us."

"I didn't realize that. I know how much she likes you two. Maybe she just doesn't know what else to talk about with you. I'll mention this to her, but I won't say it came from you."

You'll both walk away from this conversation with a sense of having been validated. Your child feels that you've taken his comments seriously, and at the same time, you have not diminished your relationship with this woman. You've also helped defuse a potential land mine.

We tend to be concerned that our kids will not like a person we date, but sometimes the opposite actually occurs: you're ready to break off a relationship just as your child has grown attached to this person. Staying romantically involved with someone for your child's sake is never a good idea. Eventually your kids will grow up and leave home and you'll be confronted with a woman you married only because you didn't want to disappoint your kids. If a relationship needs to end, tell your kids, "Jane is a wonder-ful lady, and I like her very much as a friend, but I don't think we will be happy together in the long run. As diffi-cult as it is for all of us, I think it is in our best interests if she and I don't see each other anymore."

When I asked the fathers in my survey whether they al-low their kids to impact their choice of whom they date, they were divided in their responses. Thirty-one percent say they would not let a child influence their dating choice, and another 31 percent just as adamantly say they would consider ending a relationship if their kids didn't like her. The remaining 38 percent say although they wouldn't al-low their kids to determine whom they date, they prefer getting their approval. Let's face it, it is so much easier for us to be in a romantic relationship if our kids approve. It's also easier to assess our relationship without being encum-bered by negative opinions, whether silent or vocal, com-ing from our kids.

The fathers of the youngest children, those ten and un-der, are definitely interested in what their kids have to say about their dates. Thirty-one percent would end a relation-ship if their kids didn't like her, and another 43 percent say that although their kids' opinion wouldn't affect a deci-sion, they do prefer their approval. This makes sense when you consider that at this age—rather than with soon-to-leave-home teenagers—Dad's lover could easily turn into a live-in girlfriend or stepmom. Only 26 percent of these dads wouldn't allow their kids to have any bearing on whom they date.

Perhaps in light of the challenging needs of adolescents, 42 percent of fathers of kids age eleven to fourteen would actually consider ending a relationship if their child didn't like the woman. Another 29 percent say that although they wouldn't let their kids' opinions affect their choice of a dating partner, they would prefer their approval. The remaining 29 percent of the dads say they would not allow their kids to influence their decision at all.

It's no surprise that the fathers of teenagers don't seek their kids' approval. In fact, more than a third (39 percent) say it's entirely their decision to date someone. Only 28 percent say they would consider ending a relationship if the kids didn't like their girlfriend, and another third (33 percent) say they prefer their kids' approval but it has no effect on their choice.

Even Nancy, who often challenges her dad, agrees that she should not have the right to tell her dad whom to date, but adds, "I do think he should ask me what I think of her."

Oh well, for Nancy's dad, it's a start.

Now, while you may be wondering what your kids *really* think of her, it should occur to you to find out what she *really* thinks of them. The children of the men I have dated have run the gamut from sweet and engaging to rude and unfriendly. In every case, their father assumed I liked his kids.

In the early stages of a relationship, a woman has nothing to gain by critiquing your kids or the way you parent them. I know a very attractive woman who has dated hundreds of single dads over the years. Unfortunately, she's never able to conceal her true feelings about their kids for more than a few dates. Consequently, none of her relationships has lasted more than a month.

In order for a relationship to progress, you have to open the proverbial can of worms and ask your girlfriend what she thinks of your children. If she has tried her best to befriend them by being attentive and caring while being appreciative of your obligations—and they still are kicking her under the table—she has every right to tell you the truth. It's practically impossible not to be defensive when someone maligns your children, but if she matters to you, hear her out. It's conceivable you've been oblivious to the tension between her and your kids, and this is your opportunity to uncover any problems and then do your best to rectify them.

If, however, you really believe your kids are kind to her and it's more a matter of your girlfriend being impatient with them or jealous over their connection with you, then you will have to reconsider this relationship. It is very likely not going to last. Any woman who loves you has to, at the very least, like your kids.

Try also to determine whether it's your children she doesn't like or just the way you're raising them. Maybe your kids are rambunctious, noisy, and inquisitive, which is fine with you, but she expects them to be calm and quiet and to speak only when they're spoken to. If she wants to remain in a relationship with you, she may have to expand her view on appropriate behavior for children. Then again, so may you.

It's not unusual—in fact, you might even say it comes with the territory—for single parents to be judged on their parenting skills. (This infuriates me, by the way—you'd think *their* kid never talked back.) Any woman you date is obviously assessing the way you parent. Until your relationship turns serious or unless an issue directly affects her, she should refrain from commenting on the way you're raising your kids. She can tell your son to keep his feet to himself, but she shouldn't question your decision to let him sleep with a light on.

The Ex: Exacerbating and Exhausting

One of my favorite dates was with a guy who had left his ex-wife back in Maine, hopped onto his motorcycle, and with only a bulging backpack on his shoulders headed south for good. The split was clean and fast with no tendrils connecting him to his ex. She moved on with her life and so did he.

His clean break was possible because they had no children. By contrast, the romantic relationships of most single dads, in one way or another, are affected by the mother of their children. Even if you and your ex-wife get along, she can still, in subtle ways, affect your relationship with a girlfriend. If, for example, you and a date are in the car headed to the movies and your ex-wife calls your cell phone to say her car has broken down, what do you do? Your first course of action is to tell her to call one of her friends to pick her up. Okay, but then she says the kids are with her and they're late for a party. Now what? You don't want to disappoint your kids, so you explain to your date how sorry you are but you need to take a quick detour. Make certain you offer to go to a later show or to a bar to hear music—something that will salvage the evening and make it up to her. Then, the next time you speak to your ex-spouse, tell her to call an auto service if this should happen again (buy her a membership if necessary). Just like when your two-year-old gave up the crib for a bed, your ex-wife will have to adjust.

While it's wonderful for your children for you to maintain a good relationship with your former wife, it can be irritating to your girlfriend. When you spend time on the phone with your ex-spouse, or at her house when you drop off the kids or fix her leaky toilet, your girlfriend will feel even more of an outsider than she already does. Remain friendly with your ex-wife by all means, but never keep her first on your speed dial.

A woman who dates a single father expects to get to know and eventually care about his children. But she doesn't bargain for an ex-wife. I was seriously involved with a man who had no boundaries regarding his former spouse. During one heavy downpour my basement flooded. I tried calling him but couldn't reach him at home or at his office. As it turned out, he was busy consoling his ex-wife over a breakup with her boyfriend. I was happy to let her return the favor to him.

If you and your ex-wife do not have a good relationship, then she very likely grabs every opportunity to criticize you and your girlfriend in front of the kids. Even if your children know that she is disgruntled, they can't help being influenced by what she says. How could they possibly like your girlfriend if she is described as a "home wrecker" or "gold digger"? They can't. But you can't stoop to that level, either. When two parents involve their children in their sparring, the ones who suffer are the kids. If at least one parent—and in this case, that would be you—can rise above this by being civil and compassionate, the children will feel more secure. And if you remain connected to your kids, supportive of your girlfriend, and (as hard as this is) benevolent to your ex-wife, your children will eventually see through her antics.

I ran into a friend whose husband left her and is currently living with a woman he's been seeing for three years. My friend, who is not involved in a relationship, is friendly to her ex-husband and to his new girlfriend. They attend all family functions together. I asked her how she does it. "I realized that I could be dealing with a lot worse, and she realizes that she could be dealing with a lot worse," she says. "So we may as well deal." While her ex-husband reaps the benefits of his former wife and current girlfriend being cordial, most important are the positive reactions of their kids.

I know this is easier said than done. If you have been hurt by an ex-wife who cheated on you, it can be nearly impossible to be civil, let alone friendly. If you're still angry, talk to your friends or a therapist and try to remember that your kids are in the burdensome middle position. If either parent shows resentment toward the other, the kids will be crushed—and in the end they will sabotage (even if unwittingly) any new relationship you hope to establish. They need an anchor, a strong parent who won't be so focused on retaliation that he or she starts to act, or date, for that matter, irrationally.

According to Dr. Halpern, this animosity toward your ex often manifests itself as "revenge dating." He says that sometimes men feel the need to prove themselves again as worthy dating material, so they date indiscriminately. One such man I know keeps a brag book with a running tally of more than a hundred women he's slept with. He wakes up next to women whose names he doesn't even know. He doesn't care as long as the pages of that book fill up and he can feel he's somehow getting back at his wife for leaving him. At fifty-three, he is struggling with his masculinity and his aging.

Dr. Halpern says, "A lot of men who find themselves revenge-dating need to prove something. They are often in their fifties dating twenty-year-olds just to have sex or to have something on their arm that they think will hurt their ex-wives."

Jim is a good example of this. Describing himself as a "let's-get-rocking, type A kind of guy," he was nearly forty when he and his wife of twenty years, the mother of their three kids, started to drift apart. While he was fantasizing about meeting someone new and sexy, his wife was a few steps ahead of him. When she delivered him the stunning news that she was involved with a house painter and they were planning to get married, Jim began revenge-dating, juggling several women at one time. His kids don't take his relationships seriously, and they worry about his behavior.

The social lives of the men who remain close to their ex-spouses are affected in a different way. Many don't date even though their ex-wife is either involved in a serious relationship or has remarried. Some are busy raising their kids and just don't have the energy, while others still harbor hope that they will get back together. You have to be honest with yourself about this. Warren remains close to his former wife, who has remarried. He has not entered a long-term relationship since their marriage ended, and admits that he still has feelings for her. After their divorce, she stayed in the spacious apartment they had shared and he moved into a tiny studio. Since his close quarters make it impossible to have a date over when his kids are there, during the weekends that he has them (which is often) he rarely dates.

Drew also remains close to his ex-wife, and despite the fact that she is in a serious relationship, they attend therapy jointly with their son. It's important to him that his son has a healthy relationship with his mom, of whom Drew remains somewhat in awe. Beautiful, charming, and from a famous family, "my wife was a formidable choice for me," Drew admits. "I was drawn into a dramatic vortex. I wasn't shocked to learn she was having an affair." She has just created a legal cohabitation agreement with her boyfriend, who brings two stepbrothers to Drew's son's life. "I think it's great for my son to have brothers," Drew says. "I try to be nice to his kids."

It goes without saying that if your ex-wife has happily

remarried and you are the one brooding, your kids are again placed in an unenviable situation. Remember, they want *both* their parents to be happy—if not together, then apart. So while you may have a difficult time dealing with the concept of your ex-wife dating or remarrying, imagine how your kids must feel. They know their role is to be nice to everyone involved. If you are able, like Drew, to be civil to your ex-spouse's new husband or boyfriend, you will make life easier for everyone, which—even if it doesn't always feel that way—includes you.

———

Dating may seem nearly impossible to you as you consider all the personalities that exert some influence on your social life. Always remember that you are the one in control. You may not be able to entirely assuage the negative impact of troubled children or a vengeful ex-spouse on your new love life, but your own choices and behavior can go a long way toward mitigating it.

4

Feeling Sixteen Again
Without Acting It

Admit it—all of this excitement makes you feel sixteen
again. Yet at sixteen you didn't have to tear through
your Rolodex looking for babysitters or cancel a date to
help your anxious twelve-year-old study for a math test.
You may *feel* sixteen...you just can't *act* it.

When you find yourself dating again after a long interval
of marriage, round-the-clock diaper changes, interminable
school assemblies, and heart-wrenching soccer games, you
can feel as invincible as you did years ago when you
scored the winning touchdown during the homecoming
game. It's easy to get so swept up in dating again—charged
by a surprisingly renewed interest in feeling, touching, and
sleeping with someone—that you behave poorly. In fact,
you act like a teenager at a time when your unsettled kids
need their parents to be mature and stable role models.

As is the case with a lot of newly single men, Robert's
passion-filled dating caused him to neglect his responsibilities as a father. Sex with his wife had become as predictable
and hackneyed as yet another *Police Academy* movie, so he

was dazzled when he found himself physically drawn to a woman at work. After two dates, he slept with her. It might as well have been the Fourth of July. Robert, who by all accounts is a very good dad, succumbed to this attraction, allowing it to eclipse his responsibility as a father and causing him to make a stupid mistake. He waited until late at night, when his children were sleeping soundly, to call his new girlfriend on the phone.

"What are you doing right now?" Robert asked, visualizing every tantalizing inch of her.

"Lying here. Alone. My kids are at their father's."

"The one night you're by yourself, I have my kids."

"Are they asleep?"

"Yes."

"I wish you could sneak out."

Robert thought about his kids sleeping down the hall from his room, his youngest only nine, and said, "I can't." And then he thought about the smell and feel of this woman, sensations that overpowered the good angel on his shoulder and released his unchecked, fun-loving devil. "I'll be there in ten minutes."

Taking a cue from Ferris Bueller, Robert puffed up his bedding to mimic his sleeping body. He snuck into his car, put it in neutral, and let it roll down the driveway so that the noise of the engine starting wouldn't wake his kids, then stealthily took off down the street. Minutes later, Robert was in bed with his girlfriend. They became so punch-drunk with their lovemaking they barely heard his cell phone ringing.

"Dad, where are you?" Robert's youngest daughter had been awoken by a bad dream.

"Uh, my stomach was upset. I ran out to the store to get some Pepto-Bismol," he said, relieved that he'd come up with a fairly believable excuse, but suddenly nursing a real need for the antacid.

"Then why did you make it look like you were in your bed?"

Public Displays of Affection—Yuck

Nick and his girlfriend rounded up their four children and went out for pizza. Feeling content and somewhat playful, he put some money in the jukebox and chose a song by Nat King Cole. He grabbed his girlfriend's hand and pulled her up. The two began dancing by the table.

"The next thing we knew, the kids were gone. We didn't know where they went. Eventually, we found them out by the car. We realized the dancing was affection they weren't ready for. They couldn't have been more embarrassed," he says.

This public display of affection certainly didn't violate Nick's parental responsibilities. In fact, his children probably would have been just as embarrassed had he been dancing with their mother in a restaurant. But the reality is, our kids are usually uncomfortable witnessing any affection between their father and another woman, as innocuous as it may seem. It's not just the "ew, cooties" factor that upsets them; for many kids, it goes much deeper than superficial embarrassment. Dr. Halpern says, "Holding hands and hugging is one thing, but a lot of kids struggle if the affection is more sexualized. They are very uncomfortable. Especially adolescents and young teenagers, who personally don't like all the mushy stuff from parents. Sometimes you also have to consider issues surrounding a parent's death or divorce. If there is resentment for Dad having left them or anger over a mother's dying, that can reflect deeper issues on top of the normal discomfort with public displays of affection." Knowing how to handle PDAs can be tricky. It's healthy and normal for you to show affection to a woman you care about, and your children should see this tenderness, but where do you draw the line?

As awkward as it makes him feel, Ben says he holds hands and kisses his date good-bye in front of his kids. He knows that no woman will take the place of his ex-wife in the eyes of his children, but he wants them to become accustomed to seeing his flirtatious side. Until they do, he realizes, they will continue to be embarrassed. You can't be in a relationship with a woman without touching her, nor should you be. But limit what you do in front of the kids. Hold hands, sit with your arm around her on the sofa, kiss her quickly good-bye. Just be cognizant of your children's discomfort.

Fourteen-year-old Nancy not only feels uneasy but is also hurt by and jealous of any attention or affection her father shows toward a woman. "Why do you need to touch her? Why do you need to put your arm on her back?" she reports thinking. In her words, "It's gross."

Dr. Halpern says that kids expect to see what they were accustomed to in a previous relationship. If the last woman they saw you with was their mom and you were not particularly affectionate, they may find it difficult to witness your affection with someone else. "If there was an ease of affection in your marriage, your kids will be more used to it. The ones that have the most difficulty with this are the adolescents, where it threatens their own budding sexuality. They are uncomfortable with the topic in general, and when they see it play out in front of them they find it nauseating."

The key is not only their age but also their level of sexual experience. Even if your children feel embarrassed—and they all will to some extent—the older kids (who by now are probably dating themselves) will also think your behavior is abnormal if you don't show affection to a girlfriend. In fact, as my son told me once he became old enough to date, "If you don't hold hands, I'm going to think that's weird. But I don't want to see much more than that." That may be true, but even a teenager such as Daniel, whose mother died, admits that it is still difficult to watch his father showing affection to his new wife. "I can't help but compare it with my mom," he says.

Christine, who is getting ready for college but hasn't yet had a serious boyfriend, admits that when her dad and his fiancée show affection, she feels a little uncomfortable and leaves the room. "Two weeks ago they did the arm-around-the-hip thing. I made fun of them to their faces. When they did the kiss-good-bye thing, I just left the room. I don't care if they hold hands, but my God, kissing?"

On the other hand, Justin, who is fifteen and just thinking about dating, says he can now tolerate his dad's public displays of affection as long as his dad is happy. And Sarah, who at ten has little interest in boys, observes, "Sometimes they kind of kiss in front of me. Not a big kiss. A tiny one. It's kind of awkward, but it makes me happy because my dad is happy."

Like these kids, your children will ultimately equate Dad showing affection to a woman with his being happy. It always comes back to Dad's happiness.

Under the Covers

Sleepovers, no matter how crafty you think you are at concealing your illicit rendezvous, are never a good idea when they risk making any of your children uncomfortable. After getting caught in the act by his daughter with his "upset stomach" scenario, Robert thought he had it all figured out. He would never again sneak out during the night and leave his kids by themselves. Instead, he would ask his girlfriend to stay at his house. He would very ceremoniously set up the couch in the basement for sleeping and then offer his own bedroom to her. For the benefit of his kids, she would be dressed modestly in a long flannel nightgown as she climbed into his bed alone and shut the door. Then during the night, Robert would sneak into bed with her (nightclothes abandoned) and arise before dawn to return to his acceptable spot in the basement. He performed this exhausting charade routinely...until he got caught. Early one morning before anybody else awoke Robert made his customary trek back down to the basement. A short while later, his girlfriend's cell phone rang. As she reached her naked arm over to the nightstand, Robert's youngest daughter appeared in the doorway.

"Dad!" his daughter yelled as she ran down to the basement. "Why doesn't she have any clothes on?"

Lamely, Robert told her that his girlfriend had gotten very hot during the night and had taken off her nightgown.

"But how would you know? You were downstairs!"

While trying to conceal a sleepover may make you a fairly typical guy, as far as your kids go, it is irresponsible—especially if you are operating under any pretenses that they don't know what's going on. Dr. Halpern says that most of the children he's talked to think "the excuses are lame. 'Does my dad think I'm stupid? I know what he's doing.'" He notes that it makes many kids feel powerless. "Dad is bringing someone home without even asking, and it doesn't seem like he cares about their feelings. Kids who are older and savvier say, 'Why do we have to listen to Dad having sex?' Even if they don't actually hear, they can imagine. I've never known of any kid who was comfortable with Dad's date sleeping over in his room. One kid told me, 'They play Vivaldi at high decibels and think we don't know. We know what they are doing.' Kids feel a certain level of anger about being put in that situation."

If you think *your* kids don't see through the dramatics, here's what Robert's eldest child has to say about his ruse: "Dad would make a big production out of sleeping in the basement, and she would sleep in his room. It's not like I didn't know what was going on."

Despite the fact that most single fathers go to great lengths to conceal the real intention of a sleepover, almost half the men I surveyed (48 percent) would allow a woman to stay overnight in their bedroom as long as they feel comfortable in the relationship. Another quarter of these dads say they would never allow a woman to sleep over, and 26 percent say they would do so only if they intended to marry her.

Dwight says his first long-term girlfriend lived so far away that she used to drive to his place on the weekends and stay with him in his bedroom. "After a while, my kids were fine," he says. "They were eleven and fifteen and they became attached to her because she was very maternal and stepped in to fill a void. They had no problem with her sleeping over. Well, at least I don't think so."

Dads may be more comfortable having sleepovers as their children move through their teens. Half the men in my survey who have children in the same age range as Dwight's sanction sleepovers, and the percentages increase with age. But before you consider having a woman stay in your room when your teens are around, listen to Dr. Halpern. "I think these dads are assuming a higher level of maturity with their kids and that they know much more about sex than they really do. The exposure to sex that kids get from our culture is so intense that many parents falsely assume their kids know everything there is to know. Parents shouldn't think that just because their kids understand sex intellectually, they can handle it emotionally."

Sometimes very young children can be the most accepting of sleepovers because they don't understand the bigger picture. My survey found that the majority (46 percent) of dads with young kids say they'd be comfortable inviting a woman to spend the night. It's not uncommon for young kids to enthusiastically climb into bed in the morning with dad and his pajama-clad girlfriend. You have to be careful, though, that your children aren't witnessing a revolving door of dates, uncertain as to whom they'll find when they next open it. Children can become attached easily, so unless you envision a future with this woman, don't involve the kids in these intimate moments. And while a three- or four-year-old may not understand the reasons for a sleepover, an eight- or nine-year-old has a notion. Regardless of your children's ages, it's dangerous to be cavalier about having a woman sleep in your bed when your kids are home.

"You can't send mixed messages, especially to your teenagers," says Dr. Halpern. Remember, you are the moral authority—the one your children look up to—and the example you set will likely be followed. If they see someone they respect having sex on the third date or having a different woman sleep over each week, even the most responsible kids will think it's okay if they do that, too.

Because Ben doesn't want to expose his kids to his sex life, he will not let his girlfriend sleep over until his youngest goes to college. But that hasn't stopped him from staying at her house when her teenage daughter is home. While men don't want to subject their children to a woman sleeping over, they often will stay at a woman's home even with her kids around. Think how upset your kids would be if their mom's date slept in her bed while they were sleeping in the next bedroom. Your date's children will feel the same way.

Warren understands this situation. He lives in a studio apartment and has not dealt with the awkwardness of a woman staying over when his kids are there. But his ex-wife has no compunction about letting her boyfriend sleep over. "I don't think it's healthy. I don't know if she asks the kids how they feel. I sense some discomfort around the issue with them. They emotionally run away from talking to me about their mother's relationship with her boyfriend."

David regrets his decision to stay at his girlfriend's house. The first time he did, they had just returned from dinner and a movie. Her daughter and a friend had taken over the living room, so David and the woman went upstairs. "I fell asleep and ended up spending the night," he says. "The next day her daughter was upset and gave her a hard time." David's poor relationship with the daughter only worsened, and eventually this led to the dissolution of his relationship with the mom.

Remember the Golden Rule. However you would like your own kids to be treated is how you should treat hers. If you hope to continue seeing this woman, you need to build a good relationship with her children. Your consideration of their feelings will deepen their trust in you. If you blow up the air mattress for yourself when your kids are around, then do the same at her house.

Conrad always makes sure that he and his girlfriend sleep in separate bedrooms regardless of where they are staying. "I would not want to have her kids or mine know that we are doing something they don't approve of," he says.

Until you are very serious with a woman and your kids are comfortable with her sleeping over, find other places to be together. Be creative. Go away for a weekend, borrow a friend's house or apartment, arrange sleepaways for your kids with their friends, drop them off at Grandma's for the night, or, if need be, follow that sixteen-year-old's impulse and use your car. You may feel that all of this planning detracts from the spontaneity of the moment, but the trauma of your kids witnessing you in a compromising position, though easily dismissed by you, is indelible to them.

Nancy remembers when one of her father's girlfriends stayed over. The two had returned from a night out and because the woman wasn't feeling well, her father didn't want her to drive home. "I was all right with that because I saw him pulling the couch out," Nancy says. "But if she secretly went upstairs . . . well, it's never okay if my dad was doing stuff like that."

Her sister, Sarah, remembers that night and says, "I was unsure about it, so I stayed in the room with them, but I got tired so eventually I left and went to bed. It's very uncomfortable when someone stays over."

Christine was also faced with a situation in which her

father let his girlfriend spend the night, claiming the woman had had a really bad day at work. "I said, 'Whatever. She can sleep on the couch.' He said, 'Are you sure?' They both ended up falling asleep on the couch. If she had been in my parents' room, I would have flipped my lid!"

A few months later, when her father announced he was marrying this woman, Christine said she could stay over. But she still demanded they sleep in separate rooms. "I had her booted to the third floor," she remembers proudly. "I would have kicked her out of his room if she had stayed there. It was bad enough waking up and hearing them downstairs drinking coffee. That was horrendous. I just got my breakfast and ate it on the way to school. It was really weird hearing her laugh in the morning."

In your case, if this woman is going to become your children's stepmom, you might be able to handle sleep-overs more openly. But take it slow. Let your children see her stay overnight in a different room. After several of these nights, let her fall asleep on your bed, fully clothed. At some point your child may actually suggest she stay in your bed. This arrangement may work if your kids expect you to marry her, they have witnessed your sleeping arrangements evolve slowly, and you have gradually in-volved her in your family's morning routine. In fact, con-sider a special routine when she stays over: maybe take everyone out to the doughnut shop for a treat or whip up your killer three-cheese omelet for breakfast. All of this will help your children ultimately reach a point where seeing you two share a room is normal and natural. Once this has occurred, if you choose not to lock your bedroom door, then it goes without saying you'll both be dressed in pajamas, the dowdier the better.

If your child feels like Christine, it doesn't pay to push the issue. Wait until your kid sleeps at a friend's house, or make plans for you and your girlfriend to go away so you can have uninterrupted sleepovers. It's not that Christine's dad was doing anything wrong having his fiancée sleep over in another room in the house; it just isn't worth disrupting the comfort of your child. In the end, you're the one who will pay the price.

Do As I Say, Not As I Do

Daniel returned home around midnight to find his father's bedroom door shut. Since his dad always asked his three teenagers to poke their heads in his room when they came home late, Daniel knocked once and then pushed open the door. To his astonishment, his father was in bed with a woman.

"Oops. Sorry," an embarrassed, shocked, and unnerved Daniel said as he shut the door.

The next morning Daniel woke up to find his dad eating breakfast at the kitchen table. The woman was gone. "I'm sorry for last night," his dad said.

"That's cool," Daniel said, not wanting to rehash the awkwardness of the previous evening.

"We were just sleeping. I should have locked my door."

"Yeah. Whatever."

Like so many single parents, moms and dads alike, Daniel's dad thought he could successfully conceal a woman in his room from his kids. The three boys, all teenagers, would come home late, see his closed door, and figure he was asleep. Before any of them would awake the following morning, his girlfriend would be gone.

But like a lot of dating single parents, he got caught. Your older kids are not so naive as to think your dates are platonic, but none of them wants to witness your physicality. Knowing that you stayed overnight at a girlfriend's house or went away with her for a weekend is acceptable to them because they aren't visualizing your intimate moments—and it's not in their house, right under their noses.

As a single adult, you can sleep with whomever you want and stay out as late as you'd like, but you are also a parent. If your kids catch you in the act, you'll be hard-pressed to convince them that the rules you set for them don't apply to you. So during their tumultuous teenage years, think about the consequences first and place a high value on discretion.

A few months after Daniel walked in on his dad and a woman, the tables were turned. His father had been away on business and Daniel, who was seventeen at the time, was home alone with his girlfriend. They were in bed together and they never heard the garage door open. His dad saw his son's bedroom door closed, and knocked. You would have thought they would have learned from the first incident, but like father, like son. Daniel hadn't locked his door.

"Oops, sorry," a startled and embarrassed father said as he opened and then quickly shut the door. "Keep your door locked."

Daniel's father felt hypocritical reprimanding his son for his actions, so he didn't. He acted unfazed and even apologized to his son later that day for walking into his room. Parents inadvertently communicate values to their children. You don't really want your child sleeping with his girlfriend or boyfriend, so why are you setting an example that condones it? Would you be as complacent if it were your daughter with a guy, rather than your son? As men, you often have different standards for your daughters. You probably expect your teenage boys to have sex, but certainly not your pure and demure teenage daughters. Set rules that apply to all of your children equally. And know that if you don't want your teen having his or her significant other sleeping in the bedroom at your home, then you first have to consider your own actions and behavior.

Seth won't allow his daughter to stay at her boyfriend's house. He says, "It's not even the pregnancy issue anymore. It's all the other risks, like HIV and the other diseases." He knows he has to set an example, so he is careful about overnight dates. Otherwise, he says, he'll hear, "What? It's okay for Dad but not for me?"

Let's Talk About Sex

Today's social environment for your kids is very different from what you remember dealing with as a teen. "Life has accelerated," says Dr. Halpern. "Just think of what these kids are confronted with today—sex, drugs, alcohol. On one level they are precocious intellectually, but you can't be precocious emotionally and be healthy."

Even today's middle school children have a different view of sex than you did at their age. They'll have oral sex on the school bus, casually relating it to kissing, and not considering it to be sex. The girls who are involved can be as young as ten, according to Dr. Halpern. When you date during this phase of your children's life, you make the issue of sexuality even more confusing for these already very confused kids.

That's why it is also important that you keep your own struggles with dating and sex to yourself. Your kids are grappling with similar issues, and although they may be sexually active, they are not necessarily well informed about what they are doing—physically or emotionally. Gary was stunned when his thirteen-year-old daughter asked him to help her buy a pregnancy test. "Why? Who? What? Where? I just blew up," he says. As it turned out, not only was she not pregnant, but she'd never even had intercourse. She thought any intimacy could result in pregnancy.

As uncomfortable as it is to have discussions about sex with your adolescents and teens, it's vital that you do. They all think they know a lot about sex because they see simulations on television and in movies, but, as in Gary's daughter's case, they are often misinformed and too embarrassed to ask you for clarification. Dr. Halpern says there is no reason a father shouldn't talk to his son about sex. Girls, as we discussed earlier, would be much happier talking about sex with an older, trusted female. Regardless of whom your children confer with, plan for these discussions before you get involved in an intimate relationship.

Ironically, this is the time in their lives when kids are the least talkative, yet it is also the time they need you the most. Don't equate their silence with independence. They still want your advice and counsel, so grab every opportunity you can to have frank conversations with them.

Gary realizes that, like many adolescents, his daughter sometimes acts very mature, such as when she helps out with her younger sisters, and at other times she still seems childlike. When she and her boyfriend broke up, she just wanted to be comforted by her dad. So Gary stayed up all night consoling his crying little girl. As grown-up as he thinks he is, Daniel, too, resorts to being a child when things go wrong. He was shattered when his relationship ended with his girlfriend, and he relied on his father to help him get over the loss. "I was so happy my dad was there for me," he admits.

Even though your teenagers talk a good game, be aware their personal knowledge may be limited but they may be too cool to ask you for advice. So always offer it—lovingly and without judgment.

Eye Candy—How Sweet It Is

Your behavior when you begin dating is determined not just by your sneaking a woman into your bedroom when your kids aren't looking, but how you act as a man in pursuit of the perfect mate. It's your time right now to meet lots of women, and it's your prerogative to pick one based on whatever criteria you want. Just be careful if your first priority is one you know will draw the envy of your married buddies. Any woman you choose—regardless of her age and her looks—must be someone your kids can respect as well.

Dwight says he thinks "men can be pretty shallow. A woman could be the nicest person in the world, but if you're not physically attracted to her, it's hard to get past that. If you don't want to cuddle up with her, you won't even try to see if she's beautiful on the inside."

I appreciate that most men prefer the women they date to be physically attractive, but I'm not so quick to call men "shallow." You might become so distracted by a woman's beauty that you overlook her more troublesome points, but at least you're not as petty as we women are. We scratch off our lists short, bald guys who don't earn enough money and drive ten-year-old Chevys, but then accuse men of only wanting to date prom queens.

Dr. Halpern advises single dads in their thirties, forties, and fifties to make a checklist before they begin dating so that when they find themselves under the influence of a stunning woman, they can still think straight. Start considering what's really important to you. Even if appearance is first, how a woman relates to your children must be a close second. Dr. Halpern finds that the single dads he sees in therapy want to meet someone intelligent with whom they can converse. "A sense of humor is crucial for these men, and about a third want someone who is sensual—not even so much sexual, but comfortable with herself and her body," he says, while acknowledging that looks are important. "What you fall in love with across a crowded room is not a pretty brain."

This time around you may also find yourself dating much younger women—a choice that can inherently conflict with your kids' perception of you. You remember Elton John as your first concert in college, whereas your kids and your young date see a middle-aged British guy who wrote a song commemorating Princess Diana. You are who you are, so don't try to act like you're *their* age. Your kids will think it's great that you're hip enough to know about MySpace, but none of them wants you to make it *your* space.

Dr. Halpern says many kids whose fathers date women a generation younger see their dads as foolish. He says, "He becomes a joke to them. Dad is fifty-five years old and he's dating a twenty-eight-year-old. They think that's ridiculous, and they may see Dad as a lech and very much a cliché. Ironically, the kids sometimes feel closer to the younger woman because they have more in common. They can relate to her and talk to her about things that are current."

Mike's dad is dating a woman in her early thirties, closer to his son's age than to his own. Mike says he actually relates well to her. "Our interactions are stilted, but she tries really hard to be friendly to me. She obviously wants me to like her. And I do." Mike's sister also relates to their dad's younger girlfriend, bonding over makeup, clothes, and music.

Despite the Hollywood stereotype of middle-aged men seeking twenty-year-olds, Dr. Halpern finds most men are looking for someone close to them in age. In fact, according to Judsen Culbreth, author of *The Boomers' Guide to Online Dating*, middle-aged men tend to marry women within three years of their own age. "Boomers want to be with someone who remembers the Beatles and when Kennedy was shot," she says. A Yahoo! Personals survey also demystifies any notion that May-December romances apply only to older men with younger women. Its findings reflect that more women than men—56 percent to 51 percent—say it's acceptable for a potential date to be up to ten years younger. It looks as though Demi Moore and Cameron Diaz started a trend.

Nick says, "When I look at guys who date younger women, I wonder how they do it. Twenty-something women want to go clubbing, and I'm focused on the needs of my kids. I don't know how you can date a woman you'd have such a hard time keeping up with."

Dr. Halpern counsels a forty-one-year-old divorced man who married a twenty-five-year-old. They had little in common outside the bedroom. When he said he had to prep for a test, she thought academic; he meant a colonoscopy. "They had nothing in common in terms of intelligence, maturity, or interests," he says. "One of the things that keeps a marriage strong is a commonality of interests and a deeper love that replaces the passion that eventually subsides. A lot of the men who have suffered the loss of a true partner through death or divorce are looking for something more significant than a twenty-five-year-old body."

Drew agrees. He says if he were with someone much younger, they would have nothing in common. "I had the trophy wife. Now I am looking for women in my age range. I'm looking for a real, lovely, decent life partner. I want her to be funny, smart, attractive, and real."

Seth, who is in his forties, says, "I'm not looking for someone a little older than my daughter. In fact, I wouldn't be fazed if a woman was older than me." And Gary, still in his thirties, says he is looking for a woman between the ages of thirty and forty-five, though he adds, "Even thirty might be too young."

It's not that these men aren't attracted to young bodies. In many cases, it's what comes with those bodies that a lot of single dads aren't looking for—the desire to have more children. Most single dads in early to late middle age are not anxious to begin the process of raising kids all over again. Their days of changing diapers are finished, and they are ready to move on to the next phase of their lives.

Dwight says, "I raised my own kids and did a good job. I wouldn't want to go back and raise someone else's. I don't want to be raising kids for the rest of my life. I can't imagine marrying a thirty-year-old and raising kids when I'm sixty-five."

———

You may have just begun dating, so you probably think you're jumping the gun to begin analyzing your behavior.

After all, you're the parent—you don't misbehave, your kids do. Maybe. But when you begin dating, as devoted as you are to your children, you'll still find yourself doing some thoughtless things that could have major conse-quences for the rest of the family. And if you're protesting, "No, not me," just ask your kids.

5

Sex: The Good, the Bad, and the Ugly

One wintry evening, Jack was perusing the travel section at Barnes & Noble when he ran into a woman he had dated briefly the previous spring. They sat down over coffee and exchanged pleasantries. "How's your daughter? How's your job?" Somewhere between the warmth of the coffee and the chill of the night, they decided to go back to her house.

Within minutes, their clothes were strewn about the floor like a wind-scattered newspaper and they were groping each other on top of her bed. What followed was explosive, even more sensational than they remembered. A quixotic and exhilarated Jack rolled over, took her in his arms, and softly expressed his love for her.

"No," she corrected. "This was sex. And once again you've confused the two."

Maybe you have never been told this quite so bluntly, but if you've been dating awhile, you likely know firsthand how easy it is to mistake great sex for love. And if you have yet to discover this wicked side effect of dating as an almost-middle-aged man—no, strike that; as a man, period—then take this as a warning.

Sex—memorable, serviceable, or forgettable—is just that, sex. If you build a relationship exclusively on the strength of the physical intimacy between you and a woman, it will never last. No one keeps dancing when the music stops. And men, who are typically more easily satisfied than women (a beer, a remote, and a flat-screen television would never do for us women), can easily confuse lust with love.

Diving in Headfirst

Most of us can define *sex* and *love* without resorting to a dictionary. So why, then, does something get lost in the translation when we actually experience either one? According to Dr. Halpern, men often have a more difficult time than women discerning the difference between these two feelings. "Men tend to rush into romance. They fall into lust. I think it has to do with a need to be romantically involved. This sexual component is something they both need and feel they should have. Something is wrong with them if they don't. There is a sense of inadequacy and insecurity. Men in general are more interested in having a partner even if she doesn't treat them well. They feel that is how they are measured by others. They want to have someone to call for Saturday night."

Dr. Halpern says men often enter relationships to fill an emptiness in their lives and because they don't know how else to cope. "Women have book clubs, support groups, and other women to talk to," he says. "Men rarely have this. They get together to talk about sports and work. Women talk face-to-face. Men talk shoulder-to-shoulder."

The fact that you're a father can also contribute to a premature rush into love. Scheduling separate quality time with your children and girlfriend can really start to wear on you. You fantasize that if you bring everyone together, your kids will love her and she them, and all of your time management problems will be solved. So when a relationship swells with great physical intimacy, it's easy for you to think it's the real deal. However, once you've been married and have circumnavigated the dating world a few times, Dr. Halpern says, you should begin to realize, "You have to get out of bed sometime."

I can relate to the men who genuinely believe they have fallen in love when in fact the chemistry, or passion, exists only on a physical level. I became ensnared in this trap when I was dating my second husband. When he first confessed his love to me while in the throes of passion, I returned the sentiment. Later, I asked him if there had been any other women, besides his ex-wife, with whom he had been in love. "Yes," he said. "Three or four. I can't remember." What? He couldn't keep track of the women he had loved? That should have been my first clue. Before you profess deep feelings for a woman, take the time to process all parts of a relationship. Most men who slip into a serious relationship filled with terrific sex and little else admit that they are relieved to get free of that attachment before having made a lifelong commitment.

Dwight says he learned this lesson the hard way. After his wife died, he searched for someone to fill the hole in his life. "I got involved with a woman very quickly," he says. The sex was so exciting and new that the two continued dating despite growing friction between them. "A few years later the immediate sense of loss had subsided and I went from emotional to rational and ended the relationship." Of course, love is emotional, too, but the titillation created by sex—or even the anticipation of it—is a physiological sensation, not a profound feeling of affection and devotion. Noted anthropologist Helen Fisher has claimed for years that romantic passion actually affects our brain function. In fact, scans performed on newly smitten lovers show an increase in the blood flow to specific areas of the brain. Passion, according to Fisher, is not an emotion but a physical drive as powerful as hunger. Makes sense to me. I can't think clearly on an empty stomach. And sex, like exercise, also releases endorphins that give you an addictive high.

Jason experienced a hormonal explosion with the first woman he dated after his wife's death. The sex was so new and intoxicating that he mistakenly thought the physical intimacy, which he missed tremendously, was true love. He ignored a disquieting sense that something didn't feel right. "My first impression, my first intuition, is always right, and I ignored it," Jason says. The same thing happened to me; unfortunately for me, I married the person. Fortunately for Jason, he didn't.

Ben, who also says he fell easily for every woman he

dated following his divorce, believes that in the end, he
was lucky the relationships dissolved. In an effort to understand why he was becoming attached to these women
so quickly, he attended a divorce recovery program at a local church. "I soon began to see all the tendencies that men
have and what was happening to me, particularly how
easy it is to think you're in love." And, like a lot of divorced
men, Ben realized he had been channeling the problems of
his first marriage—shakily built on physical needs rather
than on friendship—into new relationships. Today, he
says, he appreciates the importance of being able to connect with a woman in ways that aren't purely physical. "A
good conversation is as much a turn-on as a nice body," he
says. "That has been a great qualifier for me." His current
girlfriend, whom he describes as very different from the
women he used to date, is a friend as well as a lover, and
their relationship, he adds, is "refreshing."

For many men, sex had been so lacking or so mediocre
in their marriage that when they have sex the first time as
a single man, they aren't prepared for its intensity. They
often find themselves emotionally overwhelmed by this
newfound intimacy. For the better part of Robert's marriage, he felt inhibited during sex, actually believing that
his needs and desires were abnormal. When he discovered
he could enjoy sex in ways he had never even imagined, he
felt so free and accepted that he thought it must be love.

You may enter several intimate relationships before
reaching a balanced perspective. So even if you are con-
vinced you have found the love of your life, take some

time to settle down. If friendship *and* affection are present, then you've got a good thing.

Dr. Halpern says, "When you think a woman is 'the one,' you'll naturally start talking about issues that will affect your future together, such as money and children. One couple I've worked with were very much in love physically until she said she wanted another child and he didn't. There was no compromise for that. You can't have half a kid. Once these deal breakers are discussed and you both take a step back, the relationship usually ends if it is nothing more than great sex."

Since sexual intimacy is a necessary and rewarding part of every relationship, it is imperative you discern the difference between infatuation and love before involving your kids. It is an extraordinary feeling to fall in love again, to have every thought filled with her image, to spend every waking moment wanting to touch her face and stroke her hair. You can't keep your hands off each other. Your kids are probably witnessing your stupor and fearing you've lost your mind. Remember, a healthy relationship must include mutual trust, honesty, and respect, and there is no compromising on these ingredients. Great sex is merely the icing on the cake.

Now if great sex is all you want—and that's certainly your prerogative—do not introduce her to your kids. They should not be privy to a relationship that's purely physical, and has no chance of becoming meaningful. This desire for no-strings-attached sex, by the way, isn't exclusive to your gender; think of Samantha on *Sex and the City*. Women have come a long way, baby, and especially after one long-term commitment, not all are looking for a permanent relationship. And trust me, these women will never introduce their "sex buddies" to their children.

Although "hooking up"—a brief sexual encounter without attachments—may be acceptable to the younger generation, your kids will not tolerate it from you. Don't try to act hip by casually mentioning that you are hooking up with a woman. It will only make them uncomfortable and cause them to question your judgment. Besides, depending on their ages, a hookup for them probably means second base, not a home run.

It's also perfectly acceptable to delay having sex while nurturing a budding friendship. Remember how dating was when you met your first wife? Regardless of the decade, it's a good bet that you weren't climbing into bed on the first date. Sometimes it's actually nice to get to know someone before having sex. Jason says he finally understands that. After his first intensely sexual relationship ended, he still continued to disregard his hunches and confuse sex with love. He was heartbroken every time a woman broke up with him. But when the air cleared and those relationships were stripped of their gloss, he realized how fortunate he was to be on his own again. In fact, the breakups paved the way for him to ultimately meet a divorced neighbor. The two met for a drink, a friendship developed, and they have been together ever since.

Alan says when he began dating the woman who is now his second wife, they were both so protective of their children that they never risked getting physically involved while the kids were living at home. They would talk for hours over dinner, and continued to date other people. When they decided to go away for a weekend, it was entirely platonic. "I learned I could read a book, have a glass of wine, and develop a real friendship." By the time their relationship turned sexual, Alan knew he was already in love.

Better Safe Sex Than Sorry

Jim, a divorced father of three, interrupted his conversation with a friend about the stock market when the chatter of two very sexy women sitting behind him at the bar completely took his mind off bonds and annuities. A day later, he went on a date with the blond one and was captivated by her sultry voice. The sex was torrid and electrifying. For months, despite signs of trouble, Jim continued to date this woman. It was a relationship of passions—every time they argued, which was frequently, they followed it with fervid lovemaking. The sex was so mentally paralyzing that it didn't even occur to Jim to use protection. The next thing he knew, she announced she was pregnant, in a voice decidedly less sultry. "It was like total nuclear war," he recalls. They went into therapy to resolve their differences as he struggled with whether to marry her. He did, and after she had their second child, they divorced.

When you entered a sexual relationship as a younger man, the risk of pregnancy was your greatest concern, if not your only one. The term *safe sex,* for many of you, became popular only after you had gotten married. But now you're dating again and sleeping with women who are virtual strangers. You know condoms will help prevent sexually transmitted diseases such as HIV, and you even counsel your teenagers to use them. But do you use them yourself? Like most men, you probably hate condoms, so you convince yourself that since you've been monogamous for so many years and your new lover slept only with her ex-husband, you're both fine. But whom did her ex sleep with? Or your former wife? Or their sexual partners? Or what if she never married and has been on the dating circuit for a while? It's creepy but true: when you have sex with someone, you have sex with everyone he or she has ever slept with.

If you haven't used a condom in years, you'll be pleasantly surprised to discover that technology has decreased their thickness, improving the quality of your sensation. The U.S. Food and Drug Administration recommends that you should use only latex condoms that say on the package they are for disease prevention. Other types have not been approved by the FDA for being effective against STDs. And, while we're on the subject of STDs, now that you're dating, ask your doctor to examine and test you routinely for these diseases.

If you think, "No, not me," you should be aware that you or your partner may be a carrier of an STD and not even know it. In fact, herpes (there are 1.6 million new cases of genital herpes annually, according to medical expert Dr. Christiane Northrup) and human papillomavirus (HPV, which can give your partner cancer) can lie dormant for years, even decades. So not only may you be unaware you have it, you can be a carrier and infect the women you date.

There are two other benefits to wearing condoms and getting tested for STDs. One, a woman will appreciate your consideration and sense of responsibility, and two, you won't be a hypocrite when you insist your own teenagers practice safe sex. Robert says that almost all of the women he dates demand he gets tested before they'll sleep with him. He admits he never wears a condom because he has been "shooting blanks for ages" and has little concern that he's left unprotected for disease.

Unfortunately, too many men follow Robert's example. According to an AARP study, only 39 percent of sexually active single baby boomers use protection. This group often naively—and mistakenly—thinks AIDS affects only the younger generation. From 1990 to 2004, the cumulative number of AIDS cases in adults age fifty and older grew from 16,288 to 114,981. Even though these statistics include people affected much younger but who have survived with antiviral medication, the numbers are still staggering.

Gary says his girlfriend is only his third sexual partner. He refuses to use condoms because he hates the way they feel. "It's what guys do," he says excusably. Ben also admits he doesn't practice safe sex because he hasn't dated people he doesn't know. But when he stops to consider his actions, he realizes how careless he is. As I said before, just because you know someone doesn't mean you know their sexual history.

As for Warren, he acknowledges that he "should worry more. To speak frankly, the woman I date now insists on complete protection. Even though I haven't been sleeping with other women, she doesn't know where I've been the past five years. I've been tested a couple of times. As far as I know, I'm okay. Women also are more apt to insist on protection because men lose their minds in those moments."

Once Warren got used to using condoms, he and his girlfriend found sex to be natural and more relaxed, especially without the worry of pregnancy or disease. His girlfriend is smart to insist that he use protection, but you can't always rely on the woman to make this decision. Look at what happened to Jim. He didn't take the matter into his own hands, and now he pays child support and alimony.

And by the way, just because a woman is in her forties or even early fifties doesn't mean she can't get pregnant. In fact, women can become pregnant a full year after entering menopause and should be using birth control a year after they get their last period.

The Facts of Life

Sex ought to be like riding a bike. Right? So why do so many newly single men find themselves longing for training wheels?

It's a fact of life—unfortunately, not precisely the one covered in high school sex education class—that just as you begin to see inconsistencies in your ability to get and sustain an erection, women reach their sexual peak. What kind of divine intelligence came up with this plan? At sixteen you get an erection just by imagining the Playmate of the Month, and at forty you might feel lucky to succeed when a living, breathing woman lies between the covers.

First of all, you are not alone if you've had problems performing in bed. While your desire might be there, somehow, like whisper down the lane, it gets muddled along the way. According to urologist Dr. Brad Rogers, newly single men may experience performance anxiety either because they are in an unfamiliar environment or because they have underlying emotional or physical issues. He says men in their forties or fifties also have an increased risk of suffering from arteriosclerosis, elevated cholesterol levels, heart disease, high blood pressure, diabetes, and depression. These conditions, or the medications to treat them, can directly affect the blood flow to the penis and make it more difficult to get erections.

When you date in your twenties and thirties, you probably don't have a difficult time having an erection. "If you see a good-looking girl and have a slight brush or stimulation that is all you need," says Dr. Rogers. "But when you get older, you need physical contact. It has to be more hands-on. It takes longer to get an erection. Your rigidity may not be as firm, and the ability to obtain rigidity decreases. Generally speaking, erections of forty- and fifty-year-old men are not the same as when they were in their twenties and thirties. They are adequate, but not the same."

Added to this is that once you've ejaculated, your ability

to get a new erection decreases dramatically. When you are twenty, you can have sex and fifteen minutes later have it again. Now, as you approach middle age, you may find it can take hours or even a full day before you can achieve another erection. Also, once you hit your thirties, your serum testosterone decreases about 3 percent a year, and this, according to Dr. Rogers, can affect both libido and performance.

So what's a guy to do? Talk to your physician about any sexual problems you're experiencing so he or she can determine whether your problems are physical or psychological in nature. If they are psychological, you may have to explore the underlying issues first. Any anxiety can affect your performance. You may be dealing with problems concerning work, finances, or your children, and stress has a physiological impact on your body. Or you may be encumbered by feelings of fear or guilt from your first marriage. Widowed men, such as Jason and Gary, say their first sexual experience as single men was hampered by thoughts of their late wives. Gary's kids were away when a woman he had dated only twice came over to his house. They tried to have sex, but the notion that he was cheating on his wife prevented Gary from being able to enjoy the moment. "Sex had never, ever been a concern until then. I thought, 'What's going on with me?' I was only thirty-eight. Maybe I wasn't ready, or maybe she and I weren't compatible. I didn't know."

Dr. Halpern says, "A lot of widowers question the depths of their love for their former wife when they have sex for the first time after her death. It doesn't mean that at all. You can love more than one person." Divorced men may be fearful of being intimate because sex had been practically nonexistent in their marriage. It's not unusual—in fact, it is quite normal—for a guy to have trouble maintaining an erection when he has sex with a woman for the first time after his divorce. There's a lot of pressure on you to perform, while women can, as you well know, put on the performance of a lifetime.

Robert's problem wasn't performance anxiety, it was getting past the belief instilled in him as a child that having sex simply for enjoyment is ugly and depraved. His first sexual relationship after his divorce astonished him. All he wanted was to hold her hand and the next thing he knew, the attraction was so intense he felt like a sexual being for the first time in his life. After a few more intimate relationships, he began to recognize that there was more to romance than just physical contact. "For a while, I was like a body that was unable to take nutrients from food. I needed validation that wanting sex was healthy. Now I understand that a partner can show intimacy for you in other ways. It doesn't always have to be in bed."

Dr. Halpern says other psychological issues that can hamper your sexual performance include fear of rejection, ambivalence toward your partner, or self-consciousness about your body. He recommends trying some behavioral exercises with a willing partner to help you get past your anxiety. In a sensate focus exercise, you engage in extended foreplay and follow various pleasuring steps, such as caressing and holding each other. You are not allowed to have intercourse or ejaculate for a week or two. "Sometimes couples I work with come in the following week and say they couldn't help themselves, they had intercourse," he says. "It came about because there was no pressure on them to have it."

An exercise for men who have difficulty holding an erection is the squeeze method. Halpern says when a man gets to the point of excitation, his partner then gently squeezes him until the sensation dissipates. She then resumes stimulation. They continue with the squeeze method three or four times without ejaculation. The purpose of this exercise is to give a man confidence that he is able to achieve an erection. It can also help premature ejaculation, a condition that can affect men regardless of age.

"These short-term behavioral treatments can be much more successful than traditional psychotherapy," says Halpern. "Once someone is functioning physically, if he is struggling with underlying depression or other emotional issues, he can deal with it more effectively."

If your doctor thinks your problems are physical, you may have erectile dysfunction (ED). He or she may recommend several treatments, including the one most commonly talked about today, the use of pharmaceuticals such as Viagra, Levitra, and Cialis. These FDA-approved drugs differ in how long they work and how quickly they take effect. Viagra and Levitra have rapid onset of twenty to thirty minutes and can last four to five hours. Cialis claims to work a little faster and may last up to thirty-six hours. But these drugs carry potential side effects, from minor nuisances such as upset stomach or nasal congestion to more serious problems such as dangerously low blood pressure or vision loss. Certain preexisting medical conditions and contraindications with other medications could make taking these drugs dangerous, so make sure the doctor prescribing them has your full medical history. "While these drugs may work for some, they are not for everybody," Dr. Rogers says, adding, "You should never feel uncomfortable talking to your doctor about ED."

And while you're speaking to your physician about these medications, don't forget to discuss this option with your girlfriend. Your use of these ED drugs will affect her, too.

If these drugs aren't right for you, a urologist can prescribe penile injections, in which chemicals are injected into the side of the penis, and suppositories, which are small pellets placed in the tip. Because these treatments contain drugs different from those found in the pills, you may have success with them if the medications have failed.

"If none of that works, we have inflatable penile implants. We did many of them in the eighties and nineties before we had pills or shots. Although the popularity of implant surgery has diminished, it is still a good device for a man who doesn't have another alternative," Dr. Rogers says. "With these implants, penile pumps are internally placed next to the scrotum and can be squeezed for an erection." Another, noninvasive device is an external pump. With this, a long cylinder fits over the penis and is pumped to increase blood flow, which helps to force an erection. Picture—if you dare—Austin Powers.

If you do experience sexual difficulties, more often than

not your partner will be patient and supportive. But if the problem continues for a period of time and you are afraid to deal with it, then she may feel that you aren't concerned with her sexual pleasure. So if you suffer physical or psychological barriers that inhibit your ability to have the sex life you and your partner want, don't hesitate to see your doctor. By being proactive you will show your girlfriend that you value your relationship.

As you know, there is a basic difference between making love and having sex. Having sex is a physiological release that feels good. Making love involves touch, sensitivity, and verbal expression, and it doesn't necessarily turn into intercourse. It's a huge turn-on.

Middle Age or Stone Age

You've either discovered the world of middle age or you're headed there. Ten or twenty years ago you probably never imagined you'd be single at this point in your life. In the United States alone, according to *Newsweek*, there are more than 77.7 million men and women considered to be baby boomers, born between 1946 and 1964. The oldest baby boomers turned sixty in 2006.

The number of single middle-aged men and women between the ages of forty and sixty is greater today than ever before. The U.S. Census Bureau has found that 28.6 percent of adults age forty-five to fifty-nine were single in 2003 as compared to 18.8 percent in 1980. Of that number, 16.6 percent are divorced, 2.9 percent are widowed, and 9.1 percent have never been married.

As a boomer who is a dating single dad, you are a trail-blazer. Just a generation or two ago it was more acceptable to remain in an unhappy marriage than go through a divorce and find someone new. If you became widowed after your kids were grown, you probably never remarried. There were fewer opportunities to meet single women back then. Today, if you want to date, there is very little excuse not to meet women. In fact, according to an AARP survey, up to 70 percent of single baby boomers date. And we're not just talking about companionship. Some 45 percent of men and 38 percent of women in that middle-age bracket say they have intercourse at least once a week.

And if you are not looking for marriage and for now just want to have fun, you will find many women your age feeling the same way. In 2007 the Census Bureau reported the landmark news that more women are living without a spouse than ever before (51 percent). For the first time in history, single women outnumber married women in the United States. That should be encouraging news to a dating man! These figures include younger professional women waiting longer to get married than in previous generations, as well as a growing number of middle-aged divorced or widowed women who are enjoying their independence and choosing to remain single. The AARP survey of single baby boomers also found that only 14 percent of the women dated to find someone to live with or marry.

So just because you are getting older is no reason to avoid romance, especially when you consider the number of available women out there.

Feeling Sexy When You Snore or Have Other Annoying Habits

Some men fear getting involved intimately with a woman because they have problems when they sleep, or try to. They snore. They get up during the night to go to the bathroom. They grind their teeth. They toss and turn.

Okay, you just described women.

As uncomfortable as you might be with your sleeping habits, it's very likely that the woman you're seeing has similar concerns. As you may have learned in your first marriage, men aren't the only gender that snores. Even young women in their twenties sometimes need a nudge to flip over to their sides. In fact, at least 35 percent of women, regardless of their age, snore. The numbers may be higher. A single woman may not have anyone around to tell her she snores. If the tree falls in the forest and no one is around to hear it . . .

Even if your situation is severe—perhaps you suffer from sleep apnea and require external help in order to sleep soundly—be up-front with your new partner before spending the night together. Let's say you use a CPAP—a continuous positive airway pressure machine that blows air through your airways to keep your throat open while you sleep. It's better to explain beforehand rather than when she is in your bedroom and is surprised to discover you need such a device.

Gladys had begun dating a charming, good-looking man she had met online, and the relationship was going along quite nicely until he invited her to his home. On a tour of his house, she spotted what she thought was an oxygen tank behind his bed. Too polite to question him about it, she imagined all sorts of horrible scenarios. What if he had emphysema? Or lung cancer? On the next date he asked to stay at her house. As he unpacked his portable CPAP machine, he explained to Gladys that he slept with a small mask over his face that enabled him to breathe quietly, without snoring. Relieved, Gladys thought nothing more of his sleeping needs.

If snoring is a source of embarrassment for you, but you don't want to use a CPAP, you might ask your dentist to fit you for a less burdensome orthodontic device—similar to a mouth guard athletes wear—that opens your airway by advancing your lower jaw. Dr. Howard Rosenthal, a dentist who frequently treats patients who snore, says, "These devices decrease the noise generated by the air being forced through an insufficient opening. They really work. Plus it's a lot easier to pack one of these in an overnight bag."

Other simple treatments for snoring include using nasal strips—the ones that often grace the noses of football players—to open your nasal passages and increase your intake of oxygen; or avoiding sleeping in a supine position by placing a tube sock filled with tennis balls or an elongated cushion at your back. You should also be aware that snoring is often worse if you are overweight or have had too much alcohol.

Suppose you don't snore but tend to get up frequently

during the night to use the bathroom. Prostate problems increase as you age, so men often find themselves needing to urinate more frequently. (This may happen to women, too, especially if they've been through childbirth.) Just be quiet and she'll stay asleep. Parenthetically, if you do find yourself going too frequently to the bathroom, you know without my telling you to get checked by a doctor.

If you sleep poorly, be considerate of your partner. Don't wake up at 3:00 A.M. and flick on the light, read the newspaper, and crunch potato chips. If you can't sleep, quickly escape to another room and read a book or watch television. So long as you are there to kiss her good morning, she won't care—or even know—where you end up spending the night.

Breaking Up Is Hard to Do . . . After Sex

I confess, I am a wimp. I hate to break up with anybody. When my hairdresser of several years highlighted my hair so much its texture went from silk to suede, I gave her a measly tip and never went back. When my pharmacist erroneously handed me a prescription for pregnancy vitamins when in fact I had ordered birth control pills, I responded with silence to his laughing apology and took my business elsewhere. And when my dry cleaner left a few too many wrinkles in my winter coat, I drove to his competitor, inadvertently leaving my coat behind, enshrouded in plastic forever. I am not good at doling out rejection.

So it's no wonder that I stink at breaking up with guys. I have on more than one occasion shamefully failed to return their phone calls or, worse, left a "Dear John" message on their voice mail. I'm not proud of my inability to confront a date, and I encourage you—in fact, beseech you—to do as I say and not as I do.

My research for my book on single moms revealed that women generally have an easier time than men suggesting a breakup. Perhaps it's because we have a lot more practice talking about personal issues. We have no compunction confiding in our postal carrier or a stranger on the bus about our hot flashes or weight worries, while men tend to be more guarded and reserved even among their closest friends. (Case in point: watching the TV chatfest *The View* is entertaining to women but an existentialist hell for men.)

If you have had only one or two dates, you may choose to simply stop any further contact—no calling or e-mailing—as a way of breaking off any possible relationship. Or say something simple such as "We're not clicking" or "We just don't seem compatible."

However, once your relationship becomes sexual, acting like you've disappeared off the face of the earth—nearly impossible these days, when there are more ways of messaging than Morse code—is *not* an option. If you choose to end it, you're obligated to give her an explanation and to deliver it in person. Your conversation could go something like this: "You have been such a significant part of my life for four months now, and I will always cherish our friendship, but our differences just keep getting in the way. I've thought about this a long time and I don't think it's fair if I keep you from meeting someone else." Or you can use my personal—and cowardly—favorite: "I realize I'm just not ready for a serious relationship." Perhaps it's too soon after your divorce or wife's death or your last breakup for you to be romantically involved.

Even if your children contributed to the breakup—maybe they never liked her—don't use them as a reason for your ending the relationship. It should be about you and her.

Robert admits that he has a difficult time breaking up with a woman but knows it is his responsibility to do so gracefully. "I suck at it. I went to one woman's house. It took me two to three weeks to get the nerve. I run through the script. I'm sweating when I knock on the door. There's tears and crying and I keep putting the blame on me. 'I'm not ready for a serious relationship,' I say. 'I thought I was but I'm not.' I want to be kind. I try to take ownership. Always, at the end, I've been able to tell the woman what I appreciated about her." Way to go, Robert.

Dr. Halpern says, "The women I've talked to say they would rather be told up front, even if it stings a little. It is torturous to go on assuming someone likes you when they don't. Once you are on date number seven, someone is going to become attached. By then, a woman may be falling in love with you. When you finally break the news that you've been feeling this way since date number three, she'll say, 'I wish you'd had the courage to tell me then.'"

Once a woman with whom you've been intimate begins to lose interest in you, she won't let the relationship ramble on without giving you some idea of her displeasure and distancing herself physically or emotionally. Men, on the other hand, according to Dr. Halpern, often "just can't break it off for whatever reasons, and wait for the woman to break up first."

Ben and Dwight are guilty of this. Neither of them calls back if he's not interested, and expects the woman to take the hint. Dwight describes himself as the "world's worst breaker-upper." When he wanted to end his first serious relationship, he just walked out the door and never returned. When the woman didn't call him afterward, he figured that she didn't care that much, either. "I don't like confrontation when it comes to relationships. Because if someone asks 'Why?' you might have to say something that you don't want to tell them personally. I can't say 'You're not what I'm looking for.'"

You should never end a relationship by saying something hurtful. Put the blame on yourself. You're the one with issues. You can be honest without being cruel. One single dad I know broke up with a woman by telling her "You're not what I'm looking for." When she insisted he tell her what it was he didn't like, he said, "This is going to sound silly, but I have difficulty with the way you chew."

When you fall in love with someone, you barely notice these sorts of habits. When a friend of mine found herself interested in a man after her divorce, she asked me how she would know when she was in love. I asked her if he had any annoying habits. "He has a nervous laugh," she said. I told her, "When his laugh no longer bothers you, you'll know you're in love." A couple of months later I asked her how the nervous laugh was going. "What nervous laugh?" she asked.

Jason says he will not end a relationship unless he has someone waiting in the wings. "I will stay with someone if I'm miserable. I don't end relationships. I just go along," he says. He also blames himself if a relationship isn't going well. "I assume it's me. I think something's wrong with me." He continued dating one woman for months because he lacked the courage to end it.

If you're too nervous to initiate a breakup with your current girlfriend, you should understand that you're not doing either of you any favors. Not only are you miserable, but she probably is, too. And to some extent, so are your kids. If Dad is unhappy, they will sense it even if you never mumble a word.

When a relationship ends, either by your or her initiation, you have to tell your children. They don't need or want details, but they do want an explanation they can comprehend. Just tell them that she was a very nice woman but you had a lot of differences and didn't want to waste each other's time. Saying nasty things about her will only reflect poorly on you. Inform your children that you aren't finished with dating. Let them know that you've learned a lot from this relationship and will be able to approach a future one with your eyes wide open. This reassures them that Dad won't remain with a woman he doesn't feel is right for him—and for them.

The physical side to any relationship can be both thrilling and intimidating. Just be prepared for the strong feelings you will most definitely experience and the ways they may blur your good judgment. You don't want to be careless in situations that could impact the rest of your life. And you also shouldn't let any sexual problems stop you from enjoying intimacy. Help is available if you need it. So be smart, be safe, and by all means, enjoy rediscovering sex.

6

You're Not Bringing *Her* to My Game

When I first began dating, my ten-year-old daughter intentionally avoided meeting my dates by scheduling sleepovers at her girlfriends' houses or, if trapped at home, miring herself into her bedroom. I never insisted that she come downstairs to meet the men. My son, who was six at the time, would hang out in the living room, sometimes answering the door. It's not that I had an exceptionally proper son; it's that he was hopeful that every man I dated would be like Joseph. Early on, ponytailed Joseph with his pierced ear showed up in his tiny convertible bearing small gifts for my kids. In my son's eyes, he set the bar for all subsequent dates. It didn't matter what Mom thought of him.

Just when you think you're getting into the swing of dating as a single father and you've found someone special, along comes the most challenging step of all: bringing together your girlfriend and your kids. Prepare yourself for overhearing strangely foreign words spew from your children's mouths as though (you can only hope) they are possessed: "Bitch. Bimbo. Slut." All words specifically chosen to describe your new girlfriend—the woman who they think will entice you to abandon them, and replace their mother.

To ensure this doesn't happen, you need to hone your diplomacy skills while simultaneously remaining sensitive to everyone's needs: your children's, your girlfriend's, and somewhere in there, your own. Your kids' concerns are very real. The introduction of this woman into your life means inevitable changes in their lives, including—but in no way limited to—your sudden unavailability because you have a date. All the reassurances you gave them when you first told them you were dating must now be reinforced: *No one will ever replace you in my heart. No woman will ever take the place of your mother. I will never abandon you for some woman or her family.*

Regardless of their ages, when you introduce your children to a woman you're dating, they may be so fearful of change that they are unwilling to give her a chance. In the meantime, your girlfriend may try her best to befriend your kids, only to be rebuffed. The one person who can help create a bond between your children and your girlfriend is you.

A Mom or Merely Maternal?

When they begin dating, single moms often think their children are a strike against them. They'd usually rather you come unencumbered by kids, so why wouldn't you feel the same way? Single dads very often don't. Many prefer a woman who is a mother, believing she will intrinsically be kind to their kids and more understanding about the demands of being a single parent. But while single moms care very much about their own kids, and about you, they may feel that your kids disrupt their lives in ways they can't control. Single mother or otherwise, any woman you wish to continue dating must be receptive to your role as a father and the responsibilities that role brings to your life and, consequently, to hers. If you cancel a date because your child flunked his last two spelling tests and needs your help studying for the next one, she should understand. If she doesn't, well, that tells you plenty.

Nick says the fact that the woman he eventually married is also a parent made a difference in their relationship. "I wasn't dating a young woman who saw weekends as a chance to go out. I was seeing a woman who had gone through the same stages of parenting and maturity as me." The majority of the men I interviewed agree with Nick's assessment. If they are involved with their kids, they generally want to be with a woman who is a mom because she will understand their situation. Gary and Alan both say dating a mother is a priority since they will have a lot in common.

Ben says, "Dating a woman with kids makes a difference. I did date a woman who never had children. She said she understood motherhood, but she didn't." Drew says he loses patience with women who are not mothers but claim to understand parenting because they are close to a niece or nephew. "You think to yourself, you have no f——ing idea. You see your niece once a month and you have no clue what it's like to be with a child twenty-four hours a day. It's just not the same. I think women who have children are less selfish."

While a single mother may understand your role as a parent, she can also be more threatening to your kids by giving the impression she's taking the place of their mother. You can intervene here, reassuring your children that although she cares about them very much, she has no intention of replacing their mom or usurping her role. They may also feel intimidated by the presence of her children. Listen to your kids' concerns, and if you find them to be founded, address them with your girlfriend. Any issues that can be resolved early on will undoubtedly affect the happiness of both families.

Some single dads say they date single moms because they presume these women will be less anxious to get married since they already have a family. "The women I've dated who don't have kids have expressed a desire to have them, which ends up being a problem," says Warren, who's beginning to think he ought to be dating mothers. Just remember to be fair and up-front with any woman you date. If you are not interested in marriage or having more children, you should tell her from the get-go. While this choice is yours to make, her choice should be whether to leave or stay in the relationship.

Some dads I talked to say they don't necessarily look to

date mothers and are equally comfortable seeing women without kids. "I realize a woman who is not a parent won't understand the amount of time I spend with my kid's activities," Seth says. "But I also don't know if I will ever meet a woman whom my daughter would look at as a replacement for her mom. I'm not looking for a mother for my kids. One, they don't need it. Two, they have me."

Jim has no interest in dating a woman who has children. "I don't want to deal with a woman who's got a serious burden. If she's got kids and loves them and they're well adjusted, especially if they're older, that's fine. But I'm fifty-three years old. Do I want to buy into something where I'm responsible for young kids?"

If you assume a mother will be more receptive to your children, you might also erroneously assume a woman who isn't a mother won't be. A single woman who doesn't have kids might have a lot of patience and compassion for yours because she's not drained by the demands of her own. After all, a woman doesn't necessarily have to be a mother to be maternal.

Close Encounters of the First Kind

There comes that time in every relationship when you'll have to introduce her to your kids. When I asked the dads in my survey at what point would they do this, more than half, some 55 percent, said not until they thought it was becoming serious. For the most part, fathers are reluctant to introduce dates to their children. They want to avoid the fireworks if she and their children don't mesh, and they hope to avert a heartbreaking attachment between her and the kids if the romance ends.

Or perhaps, like a lot of men, they believe that the act of introducing their kids to her implies a serious commitment, much the way intentionally stuffing a blank check into your wallet before visiting the Toyota dealer signals that you're ready to buy.

So how do you know when the time is right for everyone to meet? Dr. Halpern says, "Don't involve your children unless you have a really good feeling that it has the potential to be something permanent, something significant. As a child therapist, I think about the consequences to the children. If I introduce this woman to my children, what are they going to go through? Is this someone they will like and will then experience another loss if it ends? Will it generate feelings of insecurity, guilt, and torn loyalties? I tend to be conservative by being a little more cautious. I think dads should wait a little longer to introduce them, somewhere between the couple agreeing to be exclusive and their fantasizing about a future together. Somewhere in there, it's healthy to introduce the children."

Even if you choose not to introduce a woman to your children just yet, that doesn't mean you won't discuss her. It's perfectly fine, and very helpful to your children, if you tell them about your plans to go out with her. Even if your children ask, "Is she your girlfriend?" (remember, kids consider someone a boyfriend or girlfriend if they share a Pop-Tart on the bus), you can answer, "No, she's just someone whose company I enjoy."

Drew informs his son about his dates but he has yet to bring anyone around for him to meet. "He wants me to be with somebody, and yet he probably doesn't," Drew says. "I tell him I'm not going to introduce him to somebody until it's someone who means something to me. At this point, he hasn't met anybody."

In David's case, he was prepared to introduce his current girlfriend to his children, but she suggested they wait. His youngest child remained so troubled by her parents' divorce that introducing her to her father's girlfriend at that time would have been disastrous. "I wanted them to get to know her. But my girlfriend was cautious. She said it wasn't the right time. That's been good wisdom."

Since an introduction constitutes a significant development, your girlfriend may feel your relationship is still too tenuous for either of you to meet the kids. She may be worried about her own children's reaction, your kids' feelings, or she's just unsure about taking the next step. If she suggests waiting to bring the kids into the equation, you should ask why.

Your children may not be ready to meet her if they are going through a particularly rough adjustment to your newfound love life. Work on their issues first. They process this new family dynamic at a slower speed than you do and may need additional time or counseling before they are ready and willing to meet a girlfriend.

Sometimes an introduction can't be avoided, especially if your children live with you full time. A dad who shares custody can easily go on a date when his ex-wife has the kids, but you must make arrangements for someone to watch yours. Since my dates usually picked me up at home, my kids frequently (but briefly) met men that I dated. Jason, who is also widowed, says his three sons meet all of his dates because "it is just easier than concealing them." As long as you're not opening a revolving door of dates, a spontaneous and brief introduction to a woman you're having a night out with and may not see a second or third time is appropriate. However, inviting this casual date to a family dinner or special event is not.

The ages of your children may also impact the timing of the introduction. Since very young children, aged ten and under, can become easily attached, only 20 percent of the dads in my survey say they would introduce a woman to children that age early on, and 60 percent say not until the romance turns serious. Dads with adolescent children, recognizing that that is a difficult age even in intact families, are less likely to introduce a date immediately. Seventy-seven percent of them say they would have to be serious. Not surprisingly, fathers of teenagers are a little more ambivalent; 34 percent say they would introduce a woman immediately, and 40 percent say they would wait until they were serious. Of course, these children tend to have busy social lives themselves and aren't necessarily anxious to spend any time with Dad, much less with his date.

Choosy Kids

When the time comes to introduce a girlfriend to your children, don't force the issue. If they are reticent, as my daughter was when she was young, let it go for now. Then when you think the relationship is getting more serious, you can gently but firmly initiate a meeting. Tell your children:

"I'm dating this woman who is very nice, and she would like to meet you."

"No thanks."

"I understand your reluctance. But I have given this a lot of thought. I like this woman very much and it would be awkward for you if I keep dating her and you're not involved. You mean too much to me to be excluded."

No kid wants to be left out. And all children are curious about the person Dad is dating, even if they don't admit it. Careful prodding on your part will ultimately result in a meeting.

Dr. Halpern says, "It's in part a sales job that dads have to do. Tell your kids you've met someone really special. You have a lot in common. Talk about the person's attributes and what you enjoy together. Be very forward-thinking; set a tone with positive expectations. Say, 'I hope when you meet her you will like her, too. Perhaps over time you will like her even more.'"

Sarah, who says she meets all of her dad's dates, remembers the first time her father introduced her and her siblings to a woman. He invited her over to the house but told his children ahead of time that if they didn't want her to come, he would call her back and cancel. "I said it was okay. If I said I didn't want to meet her, he'd be a little disappointed, though he'd understand that we just weren't ready." In fact, even though she was a little reluctant at first, she admits, "I kind of wanted to know the person my dad was dating." Justin agrees. He says, "I want to see who my parents are picking."

Robert has made a point of introducing his children only to long-term girlfriends. And he always asks their permission. The first time they met a woman, he asked if he could invite her to visit them for a day at the beach. His three kids (there's safety in numbers) acquiesced. In time, they became so fond of the woman that when she and their dad later broke up, they were extremely disappointed. Consequently, Robert was reluctant to introduce them to his next girlfriend. "I saw how upset the kids were when I ended it with the first woman. I didn't want to do that to them again."

You must weigh the consequences of whether to keep your social life separate from your children or involve them at the risk of disappointing them later. But in the end, all relationships require taking a risk, and there is nothing unhealthy about your kids seeing that.

It's important that you at least offer your children the opportunity to meet the woman you are seeing, regardless of what you expect their response to be. Mike is still upset that his father was seriously involved with a woman for two years before he introduced her to him and his sisters. "I know my mother specifically asked him not to introduce me to any of his dates unless he decided that they were going to be important in his life," he says. "She didn't want him bringing his random dates home. He interpreted it to mean that he shouldn't introduce anyone to us. He and his current girlfriend were going out for two years before I even heard about her. I would have preferred to have known what was going on much, much earlier. It felt like this huge deception that he would have something so significant going on for a full two years and never bring me into that loop." If Mike's dad had asked his children (instead of his former wife), they would have wound up meeting his girlfriend long before they actually did, and their trust in their father wouldn't have been compromised.

A lot of fathers assume their children shouldn't be part of the decision to schedule an introduction. In fact, only 23 percent of the dads I surveyed want to involve their children in this decision. There is no harm in asking: "Do you want to meet the woman I'm dating?" If they turn down your first few requests, which they have a right to do, ask again later. Because eventually, if you expect to make this relationship permanent, they will have to get together. If you have been honest and forthright with your kids, that ultimately will go a long way toward their willingness to meet her.

Meet and Greet

The purpose of a first meeting between your children and your date is fairly simple: they need to check each other out. It shouldn't be a long, drawn-out event. I once made the mistake of introducing a man to my son by going to a baseball game with him and his son. By the seventh-inning stretch, I was praying for rain.

Once you've decided to introduce a woman to your kids, you'll find yourself considering places that might be appropriate to host such an encounter. You can always invite her to your house for dinner—that may be difficult for her but easier on your kids, who have home field advantage and can always retreat to their rooms. If your children are really reluctant to meet her, this might make them more agreeable.

Any event in which the kids can act like kids—forget a formal dinner in a fancy restaurant—relaxes everyone and allows them to be themselves. Places such as the local pizza parlor or ice cream stand or activities such as miniature golf, bowling, swimming, or skating are all good choices.

Be honest with your children about this woman's place in your life. Don't call her a coworker or friend when you know (and believe me, your kids know) she's more than that to you. Christine remembers when her dad introduced her to the woman who is now her stepmom. She says, "He did the whole 'friend' thing. 'This is my friend.' Really? Your friend? Sure, Dad."

Justin says the first time he and his siblings knew about their father's girlfriend, his dad also tried to downplay the relationship. He pulled up in front of her house and told the kids he had to run in and pick up something. The kids asked whose house it was. "Some girl I know," he replied. "Now don't think about getting out." As soon as he entered the house, Justin's sister jumped out of the car, knocked on the door, and asked to use the bathroom. Justin says, "A few minutes later, when she came out with my dad, we asked her a hundred questions: 'What does she look like? What kind of hair? Did you really go to the bathroom?' "

Gary worried about introducing his children to a woman who had been sneaking over to his house several nights a week when the kids were asleep. He decided to "accidentally" run into her and her daughter when he took his youngest daughter miniature golfing. "She approached me on the course and we totally played dumb," he says. "I told my daughter we worked together. And then we kind of forced the girls to start a relationship. They actually became good friends. But the kids all still think we're coworkers and not dating." Yeah, right.

Your children know exactly who that person is you meet coincidentally at a park or in a restaurant. You may as well level with them. Say something like, "We're going golfing and there is a chance we will run into a woman I am going out with." Prepare them. The worst thing you can do is catch them off guard.

Single dads frequently plan a first meeting by including all the kids, hers and his, which can oftentimes work out very well. About six months after Warren began dating a woman, they decided to meet each other's children. It was a snowy day when the two families met at an IKEA store, ostensibly to shop. Although the kids felt awkward at first, by the time they had reached the checkout they had all relaxed considerably. Your kids are not going to get to know your girlfriend very well in a situation like this, but it is still a good way to break the ice.

You might try getting together at a mall. Plan to convene in front of a store, say hello, and then go your separate ways but meet again for lunch. It gives your children an opportunity to look over her and her kids and then regroup before actually engaging them over a meal.

An initial outing with all the children is fine, but arrange other occasions for your kids and your girlfriend to be together without her children present. While bringing all of the children along acts as a buffer, it also prevents any real bonding between the kids and the adults. For your relationship to enter the next level, she has to have frequent and direct contact with your children, and you with hers.

Dwight's girlfriend brought along her child the first time she met his daughters. His kids liked the woman, but not her daughter. In fact, though she and Dwight were becoming serious, the impact of her disorderly child ultimately ended the relationship. "I didn't want to discipline someone else's child, and I also didn't want my children exposed to a kid who had some sort of defiance disorder. I realized that as my kids got older, it would be a tough issue to deal with."

As much as we'd all like to believe that a relationship can survive outside the influence of our kids, it has to be very, very strong in order to do so. If Dwight had been deeply in love with this woman, he—and his kids—might have been able and willing to deal with her difficult daughter.

If your children get along with hers, consider yourself lucky. That will definitely help solidify your relationship and consequently your children's relationship with her. Tom loves hanging out with the older son of his dad's new girlfriend. Unbeknownst to their parents, they bonded immediately over X-rated movies they watched together when their parents were out on a date. This activity also made Tom very amenable to joining his dad on visits to this woman's house.

Your kids might be more curious to meet her children, if she has them, than to meet her. And sometimes the fact that she has kids can actually work to your benefit, especially if your kids relate or look up to them. But if your children don't like hers, they will be less accepting of your relationship with their mother. Don't force the issue if they fail to connect. If you and she become more serious and ultimately consider marriage or cohabitation, there will be many more opportunities to ease the kids into each other's graces.

As objectionable as Nancy finds her father's dating, she admits she has always wanted to meet the woman's kids. "It is nice to see what he is expecting to bring into the family," she says. Introducing each other's kids will accelerate your relationship. It may very well result in its demise. That's okay. You are a single dad and your children are part of your package—for better or for worse.

Bonding with Her...
a Little Superglue Wouldn't Hurt

So you've successfully introduced your children to her, and you're relieved that it went well. Not so fast—that was the easy part. What follows can make or break your romance. As a single dad, the critical next step in developing a good relationship with your girlfriend is getting her to bond with your kids.

From personal experience, I can tell you that as much self-confidence as your girlfriend projects, establishing a friendship with your children can make her feel quite vulnerable. And your kids know that. Some children will be sympathetic and civil, while others will take advantage of your girlfriend's insecurities. If this woman matters to you, you have to take on the role of facilitator as well as collaborator.

After the initial introduction, debrief both your children and your girlfriend. Talk to them individually about how they feel. Your kids will likely give you short, vague responses: "She's okay. She's nice. She's pretty." Don't provoke, just listen. Then ask them what sort of activity they would like to do with this woman the next time you get together. If your kids sarcastically suggest belching or dissecting earthworms, inform them that for the time being, and possibly in the future, this woman will remain a part of your life and as a result, theirs. You're not insisting they like her, but you are asking that they make a small effort to get to know her. It's also important to have this discussion with your girlfriend because it lets her know you value what she thinks and will not unduly be influenced by your children.

Your next activity together can be longer, and, ideally, will not include her children, just yours. Pick something your kids do well. If your daughter knows how to perform a double axel, go skating so she can show off in front of your girlfriend. A little confidence tends to make a person magnanimous and accepting of others. And if your method of stopping on skates is crashing into the boards (hey, works for me), they will bond over making fun of you.

You can also go out for a casual meal, attend a concert, play a board game, go to a playground, or have a picnic—anything that allows them to interact. Discourage your children from bringing along a friend. It's okay to do this the first time they meet, but after that, if your kids have friends with them, they'll have an excuse not to talk to your girlfriend.

If your children are ambivalent or, worse, rude to your date, don't force them to be together. Your kids probably need more time to adjust. Remember, they are dealing with issues of divided loyalties and abandonment, and the introduction of this woman brings all those feelings to the forefront. There will almost certainly be opportunities in the future to bring them together again. Maybe your girl-friend is a math whiz who can help your kids study for the SATs, or a wonderful cook who can whip up gourmet cup-cakes at the last minute for your daughter's birthday party. Take whatever strengths she has and subtly offer them to your kids. They will be grateful for her help and it will soften their attitude. As for rudeness, any form of it is unacceptable. Don't be reluctant to reprimand your kids— in private—even at the risk of hearing nasty comments about your girlfriend in return. You wouldn't tolerate rude behavior toward a stranger, and you definitely shouldn't put up with insolence toward your girlfriend.

Getting your girlfriend to bond with your children may not be easy, but just because their relationship starts off on rocky ground doesn't mean it has to stay there forever. As impatient as you are to get everyone to like one another, the process should unfold gradually. Let them see her in frequent but small doses. Always capitalize on her talents.

The ages of your children often correlate with how well they get along with your girlfriend. Younger children tend to feel comforted by anybody who is loving and warm and pays attention to them. She'll gain a couple of points if she shows up with a small treat. The teenage kids will be more open to their dad's girlfriend if they are in relationships of their own, but will see through any woman they consider phony.

Daniel, who is nineteen, says he liked his father's first girlfriend because he liked her kids (especially her good-looking daughter) and appreciated that the woman treated him like a friend rather than a son. But he disliked his dad's second girlfriend and was delighted when they broke up. "I went along with their relationship because my dad was really happy, but I didn't like her," he says. "One time I needed a ride from her house to a friend's and she refused to take me. She said, 'I'm not going to take time out of my day.' So she put me on a bus." I realize there is a fine line between your children expecting your girlfriend's help and taking advantage of her. But if I had been Daniel's father's girlfriend, I would have given him the ride. If you bond in the early stages of a relationship, you have the luxury of saying no down the road, just like a regular parent.

When you are dating someone, you are the one responsible for disciplining your children, as she is responsible for hers. If a situation warrants immediate discipline—your child is throwing rocks at birds—don't be reluctant to reprimand him in front of this woman. Her reaction to your discipline will tell you a lot about her parenting style. And if she's notably sympathetic with your child, she'll further endear herself to him.

Teenager Christine shows little interest in bonding with her father's girlfriend. Christine treats her indifferently while being openly disrespectful to her dad. One evening the girlfriend chastised Christine for her impertinence. "That pissed me off," she says. "I told her to relax. She told me I needed to respect my elders." Surprised by this woman's strong reaction, Christine relented. A kid who is purposely combative with your girlfriend may need to be challenged by her. If your girlfriend makes it clear that she won't accept brazen disrespect, your child may respect her even more.

The children who often have the most difficult time bonding with Dad's girlfriend are the adolescents. "The ones between eleven and fourteen are struggling with everything," Dr. Halpern says. "They are easily embarrassed by Dad's dating and are quick to dislike his girlfriend. If a woman seems too nice, they question her motives." Gary has experienced this reaction from his thirteen-year-old daughter. In response to his girlfriend's attempts to be friendly, his daughter angrily charges, "She's trying to be nice to me to get into your pants!"

If your kids say they don't like her, you need to be patient. If you and she make a concerted effort to involve them and if she is truly worthy of you (that's important to your children), they'll come around eventually. Nick, whose children have liked some of his girlfriends and are working on developing a good relationship with the woman he has married, says, "You hope this new woman in your life is one that they will learn to love and she will love them. That's a big worry when you're dating. If they don't love her, then she becomes the evil stepmom."

I realize that there will definitely be women your children won't like no matter how hard you try to persuade them otherwise or how nice she is. If they know, for example, that you left their mother for the woman you are now dating, they will not look kindly on her. Your ex-wife may have said something to your kids about this woman, and they may feel a profound sense of loyalty to their mom and hostility to the woman who came between their parents. If this is your situation, limit the get-togethers. It may take months or even years for your kids to come to terms with this, forgive you, and understand that Dad is much happier now than he was with Mom. Time, perseverance, and your willingness to hear them out will help diminish their anger in the long run.

You may also find that your children disagree in their opinion of your girlfriend. One might like her, while the other one doesn't. Nancy disliked her father's first girlfriend because she thought she was too uptight; however, her youngest sister, Sarah, liked her a lot. When this disparity occurs, it's usually because one child is feeling threatened. His or her role as oldest child, or youngest, or only daughter, or only son, will be affected by the interference of this person. If your daughter has been playing the role of Mom as Authority Figure or Daddy's Little Girl, she will be threatened by your girlfriend's new role in the family. If you and your girlfriend's actions fail to make your child feel more comfortable and secure, then take him or her to a therapist. An objective adult should be able to help your children appreciate that even though their role in the family may have changed, their relationship with their father has not.

Dr. Halpern says, "Expect your children to have some negative reactions. Take it really, really slow. Don't push anybody on your kids. Allow it to develop naturally and get feedback from the kids. Try to disentangle their normal defiance from what is really bothering them. Say, 'I know this is going to be hard for you. It's an intrusion, this stranger coming into your life. This is not something you asked for.' Let the woman you are dating know about the emotional status of the children so they are prepared to deal with the anger or coldness or rejection from the kids."

Do not be afraid to ask for feedback from your children. Sometimes when you see their perspective it is easier to understand their opposition. Gary gets this now. He had invited a single coworker over for dinner one night. After the dishes were cleared, she lit up a cigarette, and his children, who'd lost their mother to cancer, "freaked. They said, 'Dad, that can cause cancer.' I knew I obviously couldn't date a smoker. My kids were seeing more clearly than I was."

If only Jim had been willing to listen to his daughters when they told him they didn't like the woman he had picked up in the bar. Her revealing clothes and flirtatious manner repulsed them. "They thought she was too over the top in terms of being sexy." Then, when she became pregnant and Jim married and later divorced her, his daughters felt little delight in telling their dad, "We told you so."

Most women will go to great lengths to get your kids to like them but are often met with resistance. Observe her tone of voice, her level of interest, and how she interacts with your kids on her own, and give her some leeway, too. It's not easy being the lover of some kid's parent. She feels constantly under the microscope, scrutinized by your kids and by you. If you want to know what that feels like, then date a single mother.

A lot of kids think Dad's girlfriend tries to cater to them, and, as Nancy observes, they "don't mind that at all." What's not to mind? One of Nancy's dad's girlfriends bought her some fancy makeup, immediately endearing herself to her. Mike also says his father's girlfriend has tried to win his approval by being very attentive. It's working. "She is, frankly, a pretty likable person. And she's a good influence on my dad," he says.

Remember, you are the brass ring everyone is reaching for. You have a lot of control over what sort of relationship all of you will have. You need to be supportive, objective, observant, and wise—and patient, very patient.

Like a Six-Pack, Her Kids Are Part of the Package

Just when you think you have your kids' relationship with your girlfriend under control, you're joined by more personalities—her children. If your relationship has any hope of continuing, you have to develop a bond with her kids, too. Show genuine interest in her children. Ask them about school, or their baseball team, or school play. Do not compare them to your children. If her son tells you he is in the chorus in his eighth grade play, don't tell him your son has the lead in his. You can say something like, "That's wonderful. I love going to school plays. I am so impressed by kids who have the courage and talent to get up on the stage. I could never do that."

You can also reveal to a child a bit of personal information that you learned from his mom. Make sure it's not so personal that he might feel his mom betrayed his confidence. "I understand you have a football game this Saturday. Which team are you playing? Are they any good?" If you learned from his mom that he hates the coach and doesn't expect any playing time, don't bring it up. If he's the one who broaches the subject, listen and respond without telling him, "I know, your mom told me." It's unsettling enough for her kids to meet you—they don't need to feel embarrassed. You may have a more difficult time bonding with a daughter than a son, especially if you don't have any girls of your own. Don't be intimidated. If you discuss her interests, whether they are sports, travel, or school, she will be receptive.

You should show genuine interest but never "play" the kids. They will see right through your transparent attempts to get to their mother through them. If you act attentive in the presence of their mom but disinterested when she's not in the room, they'll dislike you immediately.

If you are seeing her children without your own kids present, it's acceptable, though unnecessary, to bring them a small gift. I know this sounds like a bribe; well, it is. I wouldn't make a habit of it, but every child likes to feel special. Depending on the age, some trendy candy, a small toy, or a popular CD might be appropriate.

As your relationship with their mother develops, continually reach out to her kids by focusing on their interests. My boyfriend bonds with my son over football. When a game is on, I just leave them to their testosterone outbursts. It's the perfect shoulder-to-shoulder male bonding Dr. Halpern describes. When he talks to my daughter, it's about movies and books, which they both love. Frequently, he'll find an appropriate DVD or book for both of my kids, who appreciate his thoughtfulness. If you are attentive to the children, they'll be much more relaxed when you hang out with their mom.

There will be times when your impressive efforts will not suffice. She may have a child who is so difficult, even to her, that there is little you can do. Or she may have such a different way of raising her kids than you do that you can't relate to them. For instance, you may let your kids stay up until they're tired, while she sets a rigid bedtime. Or you may let your kids have soda with dinner, while she insists on milk. As long as her kids aren't rude or argumentative, accept the differences. If the relationship turns into marriage, then compromises will have to be made by both families.

Robert and his girlfriend have very different parenting styles. Dinner with his kids is a noisy and rowdy affair; at her house, it is quiet and proper. This difference may have little bearing on their relationship now while they live apart, but if they decide to get married, they will have to make new rules for everyone.

If her child truly controls her, your relationship isn't likely to last. Jason's second serious relationship ended because of his girlfriend's eight-year-old daughter. The woman was so devoted to her that she allowed the child to rule their lives. The little girl wouldn't allow Jason to come to their house. Rather than ignore her daughter's outrageous demands or try to compromise with her, the mom simply gave in.

A fair warning though from the female perspective: if her children don't like you, you will probably not be long for this relationship. If the way to a man's heart is through his stomach, then the way to a single mother's is through her children. As my son intones, "I can always tell that guys are a little uncomfortable around me, as if they need my approval in order to date you. If I were to date a single mom, the hardest thing to do would be to win over her kids." Sons, in particular, can serve as a gatekeeper, protecting Mom from the wolf at the door.

No Way Is She Coming!

You have a date with your girlfriend the same night as your daughter's dance recital. Her mother will be there with her new husband. You really don't want to go alone. Your kids now know and accept that you're seeing her. Do you bring her? Only if your kids say okay. This is one occasion in which your children have final say. Their activities and school events are their territory. It's awkward enough that their dad has a girlfriend, but bringing her out in public in front of their friends and teachers can be mortifying.

So ask, and then respect their answer. Their response may surprise you. Fifty-six percent of the kids in my survey say they are okay with Dad's date attending their games, school activities, or holiday gatherings. Another 33 percent say it's okay as long as Dad asks their permission. Only 11 percent reply with a categorical no. Nancy and

Christine are two examples of this minority. Nancy refused to go to her school concert if her dad brought his date. And while Christine didn't stop her father's girlfriend from coming to her games, she made it clear that she didn't want her there.

Most kids, though, will grant permission if you ask them. Tom thinks it's acceptable for his father's girlfriend to come to his basketball games because the more fans he has, the better. And Daniel finds himself trying to impress his father's date when she comes to his concert. "I want to be an asset to my dad," he says.

Whether your girlfriend tags along also depends on the significance of the event. If it's a school play or a sporting event, your child may actually take pride in showing off his talents. But if it's an occasion that tends to be more personal, such as a first communion, bar mitzvah, or school graduation, don't be disappointed if your child requests that attendees are family only.

Take Mike, for example. He accepts that his father's girlfriend visits him at school and even spends holidays with them. But he thinks that if she comes to his college graduation "it would be weird." He says, "It's the culmination of years of work by both me and my parents, and it just seems a little odd that she would be there in the same sort of position. But, on the other hand, it feels fake to ask my dad to come alone."

If his father has already remarried by the time of the graduation, Mike wouldn't expect his dad to ask for his permission. Once a woman has become your wife and your children's stepmom, your kids will have to accept her involvement in family activities. And if they don't, your marriage will suffer the consequences.

It's Over—the Kids Say So

Even if we promise ourselves that we will not let our children unduly influence our choice of whom we date, we may find it difficult to stay with someone they hate or to break up with someone they love. As I mentioned in Chapter 3, my survey shows that many fathers are determined to end a relationship if their kids disapprove. Jason says he would have if he had known what his kids were thinking. But it wasn't until he broke up with the woman that his sons told him the truth. "My kids are very insightful. They saw things way before I did," he says. Drew also says he would probably end a relationship if his son didn't like the woman, but he adds, "I would like to believe that I wouldn't date someone he didn't like."

Unlike Jason and Drew, some dads say they would continue dating a woman their kids disliked. "I wouldn't date someone who was awful. But I don't think if they hated my current girlfriend that would change things. If they hated her, they'd probably hate anybody," theorizes Conrad, who, despite resistance from his youngest child, intends to marry his girlfriend.

"I think you allow yourself the luxury of believing that your kids will begin to care about her as they get to know her," says Nick. "I would not have ended the relationship if they hadn't liked my girlfriend, because you have to assume that in time that will come."

Interestingly, my survey of the children finds a majority (61 percent) say that regardless of what they think of a woman, the decision to continue seeing her should be left up to their dad. Only 17 percent say they should be allowed to decide whom Dad dates.

In the youngest age group—kids ten and under, who are still fairly unquestioning and trusting of their parents—a decisive 63 percent agree that they might tell their dads what they think, but it is his decision. Only 11 percent feel they should have final say. Not surprisingly, the largest number of kids—23 percent—who think they can weigh in on Dad's decision are adolescents, although even among them some 59 percent cut their dad a little more slack, saying they can offer an opinion but he has final say. Among the teenagers, only 8 percent say they should be able to dictate whom their father dates, and more than half (52 percent) say they might tell him how they feel though it's his decision.

David says, "I live my life. That's what I teach them. I'm hoping my daughter will be mature enough to recognize that Dad has a right to be happy. Because sooner or later, it'll be my decision."

While you might ignore your children's opinions if they don't love your girlfriend, it doesn't mean you ignore your children. They obviously have issues that need to be addressed. One of your goals in dating well while parenting well is to be a role model for your children. Even if your marriage to their mother ended in divorce, your children should know that two adults can fall in love and stay in love. They need to witness this if they are going to have successful adult relationships of their own one day.

They're Attached, You're Detached

One of the dangers you face as a dating dad is the possibility of your children becoming attached to someone that you no longer wish to date. Since you can't predict the outcome of a romantic relationship (would you have married their mother if you thought it would end in divorce?), you may discover that just as you decide to end it, she has become close with your kids. If you break up with the woman, do they deal with yet another loss?

If it's your decision to end the relationship, your kids deserve an explanation. When you dated a woman a few times and your children hadn't spent much time with her, it was sufficient to say, "She's a nice lady but we're not right for each other." Now that your children have bonded with a girlfriend and very possibly her children, they may be surprised and disappointed to learn that it's over.

Tell them the truth appropriate to their age. It may be that you had hoped your differences in interests, child rearing, or personality would have somehow been resolved, but you now realize that isn't going to happen. She's a wonderful woman but not someone you can see integrating into your family permanently. This is important. You want your children to trust your judgment and to know that their long-term happiness factors into your decisions. They obviously don't need to learn that her snoring got to you or that she slept with her boss.

Your kids may be devastated...to a point. Remember they still have you, which is most important to them. They want you to be happy, and when you're not, they know. You can't conceal your moods from your children. The kids I interviewed say that even if they miss someone their dad dated, they are moving on just fine. Justin, for example, really liked one of his father's girlfriends. "She was very nice. Our whole family liked her and we had become attached to her." But once his father broke off the relationship, Justin accepted that he would not see her again.

You may choose to allow a former girlfriend to see your kids for a period of time. If your children ask to continue seeing her but you are uncomfortable with that, you certainly have every right to say no. If, on the other hand, your breakup is mutual and amicable and you believe it will be beneficial to your children—perhaps she's been a trusted adult friend to your daughter—then you can allow it. In time, as your kids get older and busier with their own social lives, this relationship will probably fade.

Ironically, sometimes the child who resists the most when you are in a relationship is the saddest when the romance ends. It may take a new woman in Dad's life for that child to realize the first one wasn't so bad. Even Nancy, who has rarely liked her father's dates, admits that she ended up missing a girlfriend she hadn't liked in the beginning after her father broke up with her.

Justin says when his father told the kids he was no longer seeing the girlfriend he and his siblings had come to like, they were disappointed but appreciated their dad's situation. "You don't need a full explanation, but you have to tell your kids a little something because they want to know," he says.

Reassure your children that this relationship taught you a lot and you're now looking forward to meeting someone new. Observing Dad end a relationship that wasn't quite right helps your kids have faith in your judgment the next time around.

———————

Don't avoid introducing a girlfriend to your children just because you dread their reaction. If your relationship has long-term potential, it's important for them to get to know each other—sooner rather than later. Your patience and encouragement will go a long way toward helping these people you care so much about to bond. And—superglue aside—that takes time.

7

What's Next? Playing House or Getting Hitched

The two times in my life I broke the news I was getting married I had as much finesse as a bull in a china shop. For nearly four years I concealed Charlie from my parents because I knew they disapproved of our difference in religion. It was only when we decided to get married that I began sprinkling his name into casual conversation. Thinking I had laid sufficient groundwork to announce our engagement, I invited my parents to my apartment for dinner. Charlie planned to cook them a memorable meal, ply them with vodka martinis, and then—after they were sufficiently anesthetized—gently announce he wanted to marry their daughter.

Instead, I took one look at my parents standing at my door—my mom, always the model of etiquette, cradling a lemon meringue pie—and blurted out: "We're getting married." I cried. My mom cried. My dad looked crestfallen. Fortunately, my parents ultimately grew to love my first husband.

Still, you would have thought I had learned a lesson the next time I decided to get married. I had been dating my second husband for only three months when he proposed. We told my kids together. While we might have seen it coming, my kids had not. All those evenings he and I had been together and all our late-night phone calls had occurred off my children's radar screen. As far as they knew, we were still getting to know each other (given the subsequent divorce, I'd say they were right). They were stunned and distressed. He then decided to tell his kids without me. He took them to a pizza shop where his eldest child was waiting tables and, in this very public place, announced he was marrying me. Another round of tears.

About a year after that emotional evening, we got married. I had doubts during our engagement, but I was so caught up in the chaos of planning a wedding, involving my kids and his, building a house, and blending the families, the furniture, and the artwork (Don't laugh. Painted dogs on driftwood might be your thing. It wasn't mine), that I suppressed my own instincts. It was too complicated to apply the brakes, so I didn't. Of course, in retrospect, had I stopped the wheels in motion then, I would have avoided a lot of heartbreak and trauma down the road.

I learned the hard way . . . but you don't have to.

Before You Say "I Do"

If you have any doubt about whether to marry this woman, you need to spend more time with her. And the one thing you lack as a single parent is time. Consequently, it's easy to rush into marriage because you think a combined family arrangement will be far more manageable than juggling your children and your social life—flaming sticks or knives would be easier. I understand this all too well. I entered my second marriage because it had become difficult maintaining two separate families, plus it was "weird" for my then thirteen-year-old to tell her friends her mom had a "boyfriend."

It's also easy for men, who tend to be problem solvers rather than wholly emotional beings, to approach remarriage from a very practical point of view. Men may not consider the long-term implications of this woman becoming your children's stepmother, not to mention your becoming a stepdad.

Even if you feel that you have in fact found true love, keep in mind that bringing two families together is a lot of work. Make sure you prepare yourself, your kids, and her family as much as possible. Do not delude yourself into thinking the love that you and your fiancée feel for each other will be enough to sustain a blended family. Your new family will require constant evaluation, genuine effort, and significant compromise—for everyone involved.

Not all dads want to get remarried. It has become increasingly common for many single fathers to choose to live with someone instead. This has to be an arrangement you are comfortable with based on your own beliefs and, if your kids still live at home, one that they can accept. It is certainly a little easier to disentangle yourself from a cohabitation arrangement than a marriage.

Dwight waited until his youngest child left for college

before he moved in with his girlfriend and eliminated the five-hour drive between their homes. But he wasn't prepared to take the next step of marriage. "You've experienced life enough to know that love is blind," he says.

You already know how traumatic it is for you and for your children to deal with a marriage ending, whether through divorce or death. So make sure you've considered all your options before making a decision that will affect not only you and your fiancée but your children as well. Conrad did this. He promised his youngest daughter that he wouldn't get married until she graduated from high school. "Making that promise helped my daughter feel secure," he says. "Her life wasn't going to change. I didn't want to cause her any more pain than she already experienced." A few months before his daughter left for college, Conrad married his girlfriend. Grateful that her father kept his promise, his daughter willingly and happily attended the wedding.

Like Conrad, widower Seth can't imagine remarrying until his youngest child graduates from high school. He thinks a new marriage could have a "detrimental effect" on his children. It's easy to reach this conclusion when you are not involved in a serious romance. But, if your children are very young, you might not want to wait years for them to graduate in order to live with or marry the woman you love—especially if you plan to have more children together. Besides, bringing a stepmother into your home might be a wonderful addition for everyone. Just make sure that your decision to marry this time around takes into consideration not only your needs but your children's as well.

"Kids, Can We Talk?"

Remember when you totaled your father's Ford and, fearful of his wrath, you found every excuse to avoid going home? As expected, he was furious when you finally told him. But you felt such relief getting it out and in the open that you stoically accepted his punishment of being grounded for a month and doing household chores to pay for the damage.

The same feeling of dread has arisen now as you prepare to tell your children you're getting married. You expect them to react with shock, anger, tears, or, worse, an indifference that you know is cloaking much deeper and more worrisome feelings. As I've said before, never confuse your children's ambivalence with acceptance. Chances are they have not prepared themselves for Dad one day remarrying, and they may believe that if they just don't talk about it, it will go away.

The ages of your children will probably affect their reaction. Very young children, under the age of eight, can be persuaded to accept the news if you sweeten the deal with some positive changes for them. If a new marriage means a bigger house or a new wooden swing set or a cool older brother, your little one may be very happy with your remarriage. Adolescents are another story. They are already feeling conflicted about the change in the family following the divorce or parent's death. If Mom is still alive, they may be hoping for a reconciliation between the two of you. If not, they are accustomed to the close-knit family you've become and aren't looking for a stranger to intrude. Be honest with them. It's tempting to promise them you'll never sell the house or make them change schools, but in fact you aren't sure how your future will unfold. Instead, assure them that all decisions that affect the family will be made with input from them. And compromise. Everyone will have to compromise.

Teenagers can be either happy for you if they see themselves on the way out—graduating from high school and leaving your house—or miserable if they feel like they're losing control at such an important time in their lives. They are old enough to be told that you are thinking about marriage. The goal is not to invite them to talk you out of it but to get them accustomed to the upcoming change in your household. Treat them with respect and you just might be pleased with their reaction.

If you've wisely kept your kids in the loop throughout your relationship with your girlfriend, telling them you're getting married will go much more smoothly. That means that from your first few dates, you've kept them informed about your feelings for this woman and the seriousness of the relationship. Once your children have spent more time with her and she has become a fixture at your family meals or excursions, the conversation could go like this:

"Grace and I often wonder what it would be like to have all of us live together."

"What? Are you guys getting married?"

"No, not at this point. But we're thinking about it."

"What's going to happen to me?"

"What do you mean, what's going to happen to you? You're my son. Nothing will change with us. I could never stop loving you. If we do decide to get married, you'll be the first person I'll tell and the two of us will discuss it."

While you might be thinking of how to pay for a home together and how to merge your finances, your kids are consumed with equally unnerving thoughts: *Will her kids live with us? Do I have to share a room? Will we keep our dog? Will we still celebrate Christmas at Grandmom's?* Don't dismiss these concerns. Your child is feeling insecure about the news that this stranger, and possibly her kids, will now be moving into his life—and changing it—permanently. Validate his feelings, even if they seem minor compared to your worries, and promise him that at the very least, his opinion will be heard.

Dr. Halpern says, "I would say to the kids, 'I know you're going to have a whole array of feelings. Let's talk about the things you're worried about.' They will worry about the loss of Dad's love and his time. They also wonder if this new person will come into the household and take charge. The kids think that Dad will choose the woman over them, taking her side over theirs. Some of them worry about Dad being too weak to stand up to her rules. This woman will come into their house and everything will be different."

Children of single fathers fret about this more than those of single moms. They think their dad will be happy to relinquish running the household to *her*. As anxious as you will be to move ahead with your plans, be patient with your kids. Don't dismiss their fears regarding the new household rules. Most will adjust if they feel their concerns are recognized and that there is fair compromise.

Sometimes as hard as you try to reassure your kids, they may still be unhappy. Dwight experienced this with one of his children. He and his girlfriend had been dating for a year when the geographical distance between them became too much of a burden and they decided to move closer to each other. "I was running back and forth," he says. "At some point I told my kids that we were looking to buy a house because I was tired of the commute. My youngest said, 'You're not going to sell our house, are you?' 'Of course I am. I don't need two houses.' When she came over supposedly to help me pack, she spent three days in the house doing nothing. When I finally asked for her assistance, she said, 'If I don't do it, Dad, maybe it won't happen.'"

In Dwight's situation, it wouldn't have mattered how much he prepared his kids for the inevitable—his youngest child was still going to be devastated about the changes in their family. Even if you've adequately prepared your children for the seriousness of your relationship with a woman, when you tell them you want to get married, it may still come as a shock.

Or your situation might be a little more complicated, like Nick's. He says he couldn't prepare his kids because he feared the animosity between him and his ex-wife would effectively derail his plans to remarry. "How I broke the news to them is one of the things I wish I had done differently," he says, "but I don't know if I could have. Telling my kids ahead of time that we were getting married held the opportunity for all sorts of problems. My ex-wife would have canceled my weekend with the kids, like she often did if she was particularly angry. And if I had told them in advance, they would have told their mother. From the minute I told them until the wedding, there would have been a black cloud over their heads. I didn't feel they needed that in their lives."

So on the day of his wedding, Nick picked up his children at their mother's house, and as they climbed into his car he announced they were going shopping for some new clothes. When they asked him why, he told them they would be attending his wedding that night. His son balked and his daughter reluctantly agreed. In the end, they went shopping, changed into dressy clothes, and grudgingly headed to the church.

"I think I was in a catch-22 and had no good decision to make, especially because I didn't have an amicable divorce. You make the best choice you can at the moment, and that's the one you have to live with. And you pray for the rest of your life that it was right." Today, Nick's children have become more accepting of their father's marriage. They laugh now when they look at the wedding pictures in which his son and stepson are standing with their arms folded, looking totally disgusted with their parents.

Like a lot of divorced men, Nick dreaded telling his first wife that he was getting married. How and when you present this news depends on your situation. If you have a good relationship with your ex-wife, you may choose to notify her before you tell the kids in the hopes that she'll lend her support when you make the announcement to them. But if you and she are on poor terms, you may have no choice but to tell your children privately and inform your ex-wife later. If you anticipate an especially emotional or angry reaction from her, make sure to have this discussion at a safe distance from your kids. Don't call her with this news while she's in the car driving them to a piano lesson. And whatever you do, don't put your kids in the middle of this by telling them to break the news to their mom. That's your job, not something they should be burdened with.

Alan told each of his kids individually when he decided to get married, knowing that their reactions would vary. His two sons were fine. His daughter was not. "It's too soon. How can you do this to me?" she protested.

"It's always about her," Alan says. "This was my choice. I didn't ask for her approval, and I think that's part of my daughter's anger. I didn't get her permission. She didn't want to come to the wedding. It's the only time I've forced her to do anything. I told her, 'I want you to be there, and in the long run you will regret it if you aren't.'"

While you can insist your children attend your wedding and act politely, it is unfair of you to insist they play a bigger role. Never force a recalcitrant eight-year-old to be a flower girl or a disgruntled teenager to be your best man. Their level of participation should be their decision. If you suggest these roles as an option and let them know how honored you would be for them to be a part of your day, you may be pleasantly surprised at their responses. All little girls like to get dressed up, and a teenage son will be flattered if Dad considers him his best man. But remember, no pressure, and no guilt if they decline.

Jason's relationship with his three sons is so secure that they ultimately accepted, however unenthusiastically, his decision to marry a woman he had begun dating only three months earlier. He called his sons—all away at college—to warn them that when they came home for Thanksgiving break, he had something to tell them. Unable to wait, his sons insisted he reveal his secret on the phone. When he told his eldest son, he was met with silence. His son then said, "Okay, I guess you know what you're doing." When he called his youngest son, the response was more direct: "Are you crazy? You just met her and you're ready to sell the house and move? Can't you wait until I at least get out of college?" His middle son said, "It alarms me because I saw you play house with your first girlfriend. But I would never second-guess you." Fortunately for Jason, his sons have remained close to him and have all gradually begun developing a relationship with their stepmom.

Wedding Pictures and Rings: Handle with Care

When I became engaged to my second husband I removed Charlie's and my wedding picture from my bedroom bureau. It had sat there for nearly eighteen years, but like many fixtures that blend into the woodwork, I didn't think my kids would notice. Wrong. Within hours after I gently took it down and put it in my lingerie drawer, my daughter commented on its disappearance. As if my recent engagement weren't traumatic enough, it appeared as though I had forgotten about her dad.

Children of divorce expect their parents' wedding picture to be removed, but children of a deceased parent see the picture and wedding ring as symbols that Dad will never forget about Mom. They may not be able to appreciate that when you remove these symbols of their mom's place in your life, it is only because you are involved in a new serious relationship and it has no bearing on the marriage that ended tragically or the feelings you will always have for your first wife.

Christine noticed immediately when her father took off his wedding ring. " 'Where's your ring?' I asked him. All he said was that he had taken it off. I knew then that he was serious with his girlfriend."

Long after his mother died, Daniel realized that his father had become serious with the woman who became his stepmom when he noticed his parents' wedding picture had been removed. "It was kind of f——ed up. But I guess you've got to do what you've got to do. I said nothing to him because I thought it would be terrible to put him in that position. Maybe there shouldn't be pictures of just my parents together, but pictures of our family, including my mom, could be in his room. I see less of my mom in the pictures. When I'm in his room and I see pictures of his new wife where he and my mom used to be, it's sad, but I understand."

As supportive and understanding as Daniel is, he still admits, "It's weird to hear him say 'I love you' to another woman." All children, regardless of their age, feel like Daniel to some extent. The first time I saw my stepdad driving my deceased father's car with my mother in the passenger seat, my life felt unhinged. I love my stepdad, but the two people who raised me and nurtured me were my parents. Even after a divorce, your children still fantasize about a devoted relationship between the two people they love most in this world. Never minimize the significance of removing a wedding picture or taking off your ring. To you it signals that you are ready to move on, which is healthy and wonderful, while to your children it signals an ending that is dismal and entirely out of their control.

Wedding pictures have significance not only to your children but also to your serious girlfriend. To leave them up when you are remarried or about to remarry, Dr. Halpern advises, is "offensive and hurtful" to your new wife. "Fathers should give the pictures to the kids to keep in their scrapbooks or keepsake boxes so they have those memories. You're not invalidating their past or erasing their feelings, but in most new families, having the past on public display is difficult for everyone, especially the new person coming in."

You can ask your children if they would like to display photos of their mom in their bedrooms. My son has several photographs of his dad in his room. There's one of his dad as a young boy on a pony, one when he was in the Marine Corps, and one of him holding my son as a baby. I would never tell my son to remove them, nor would I want to be with a man who would insist he do that.

Dr. Halpern says, "With a divorce, wedding photos should not be on display, period. With a death, they should be allowed in a child's room. They are pictures of happier times."

Prenups With or Without the Nup

Paul McCartney must have thought all you need is love when he decided to marry model Heather Mills in 2002 in a lavish $3.2 million wedding in Ireland. Four years and one beautiful daughter later, their marriage ended. With an estimated $1.5 billion estate and no prenuptial agreement, one wonders what Paul was thinking.

You don't need to be a billionaire to consider the need for a prenup, especially when either of you brings kids into the marriage. Judith E. Siegel-Baum, a New York City–based attorney specializing in trusts and estates, and matrimonial law, recommends prenups for every person entering a second marriage in order to protect their kids' inheritance.

"Although a spouse can waive his or her right to inherit, if the parties do not have a prenuptial agreement, this issue of waiver of estate rights never comes up until after they are already married and are consulting a lawyer to prepare their wills. At that point, the rights already exist and it is much more difficult to obtain the waiver," warns Siegel-

Baum. It's a little like placing a juicy steak in front of your golden retriever and hoping the dog shows no interest in scarfing it down.

Don't perceive a prenup as unromantic, disrespectful, or symbolic of a lack of trust. Try to view it as a legal document that takes away the financial concerns common in second marriages and protects all the parties involved.

"Whatever problems you think you're going to have, you'd better take care of in a prenup. You don't get another bite of the apple. You can amend a prenup, but in order to do that, both parties have to agree to amend it," Siegel-Baum says, adding that doing so can be a sensitive issue once you're married.

There are many reasons for choosing to sign a prenup. For example, you might inherit a family business that you want to keep in your family, not in hers; you're moving into her house and you're giving up property rights (consider where you will live if you divorce); or you're marrying someone wealthier than you and making significant changes to your lifestyle. If the marriage ends, you don't want to go back to living in a studio apartment. And a lot of women today, whether divorced or widowed, also want a prenup to protect their income and inheritance for their kids.

In most states, your will trumps your prenup, so if you'd like to leave more to your spouse than is written in the prenup, you can add it to your estate plan. In fact, so long as you are of sound mind you can change your will up to one minute before you die. Good timing is everything!

A lot of single dads choose to live with someone rather

than get remarried. Some of these men, like Dwight, sign agreements of cohabitation, which can show how property and money will be managed while you are together and distributed in the event of a separation or death. "We both have significant assets," he says. "After twelve or thirteen years of being single, you're going into a relationship again, knowing that things don't always last forever and how suddenly they can change, so why mess it up for the kids?"

Philadelphia attorney Sandra Schultz Newman says that while the intent of a prenup is fairly clear, cohabitation agreements need to be more "artfully drafted." Be forewarned that most states do not recognize common-law marriages, so if you are just living together, you have no inheritance rights. That means that while in most states inheritance money between spouses is not taxable, such money between cohabitating couples is.

Cohabitation agreements also create legal issues that wouldn't otherwise exist. For example, if you and she live in your house and you leave it in your name, it would automatically revert to you if you were to split up. However, if you create a cohabitation agreement, it might actually raise a question as to who gets to keep the house, says Siegel-Baum.

Both prenups and cohabitation agreements can be written to cover very specific issues about who pays for the children. You may choose to list that you are each responsible for your own child's college tuition, medical expenses, or camp fees. Before you move in together or get married, determine how much each of you will contribute to a family account and what it covers. If you have kids and she doesn't, does she pay for your kids' clothes or activities? These are important decisions that need to be addressed ahead of time.

Whatever you decide to do, whether it's a legal agreement or some other financial plan such as taking out a life insurance policy with your new spouse as the beneficiary, it would definitely help to review the situation with a set of trained legal eyes. Because as Paul of all people should have known, you "Can't Buy Me Love."

The Brady Bunch

The Brady Bunch had one thing going for it: Hollywood. If you could write the script, set the scene, and shout "Action!" when you were ready, your own version of a blended family might go off without a hitch. But the reality is that blending two families is difficult and ends in divorce close to 60 percent of the time. To prevent this worst-case scenario, you and your new wife have to view your family as a whole unit—us and ours, rather than yours and mine. For any marriage to work, even when you share children, a couple must not only show each other mutual respect but demand it from their kids as well. If not, it's a cinch for your children to split you apart.

Children in an intact family don't normally feel insecure about their role or relationship with their mom and dad. Children in a blended family frequently do. Your task is to reassure, respect, and involve your children while being an attentive and caring husband. "A lot of times kids have emotional scars from death or divorce, and they bring them into a new marriage. Family therapy is almost a necessity to work through their issues," says Dr. Halpern. "As a parent, you need to be open to getting some feedback from your children, whether it is accurate or self-serving. It has to be an ongoing discussion. People don't take it far enough. They close off discussions when there are still unresolved issues."

Dr. Halpern says that when you blend two households, your kids are probably thinking: "'She came into our lives and everything has changed. My dad is not the same as he was before.' When they lose one parent they become fearful of the future, and some of them struggle with that even in a remarriage. 'Mom died and if something happens to Dad, I'm now living with a stepmother who is not my real mom.' If they feel that things can be taken abruptly from them, kids can become very insecure."

Regardless of whether you chose to remarry or live with a woman, your children may feel their bond with you has weakened. Be sensitive to their feelings. Although they never bargained for a new family, as your children, they've come along, willingly or not. They should see a strong bond between you and your new wife or live-in partner, but they should still believe they come first in your heart.

You are capable of helping them feel this way. It means understanding when it's important to let your new wife or your children influence family decisions. If your wife wants to pick a restaurant for a family dinner, support her decision. It's really not a big deal, but it sends a message to your children that her opinion counts. However, if your wife wants to go furniture shopping on an evening when your son has a basketball game, you need to support your son. If you have plans to go to the movies but your daughter wants you to help her buy a dress for the prom, suggest that you and your wife both go shopping with her. Use this as a guide: if you were still happily married to their mother, which activity would you choose? Back then you would never have missed an important occasion with your child. It was easy to recognize the priorities.

Daniel says that since his father has remarried, the dynamics in his family have changed, but he and his brothers still feel connected to their dad. "My stepmom also treats me like one of her own, so I'm not missing any benefits from before except for private time with my dad." It's true that once you remarry and form a new family you'll have less private time with your kids. You probably had less private time with them when you were married to their mom, too. Just try to be aware that it may be something with which they struggle.

The first decision you make as a blended family is where to live. So many issues come into play here. Is one house bigger? Is one house mortgage-free? Are they located in different school districts? Should you find a new house so the kids don't feel they're invading another family's territory? Will the kids want to share a room? Talk this over first as a couple so you have a list of possibilities that you both support. Then bring all the children together. This process is one of give-and-take: *I'll give up my bedroom if we get a pool table at the new house. I'll share a room if we get to totally redecorate it. If I can have a television in my room, I'll be happy to move.* When you involve them in the decision making, they will get caught up in the excitement of planning for a big change.

In Alan's situation, his new wife and her family moved into his home, so they added another bedroom onto the house for the boys. Christine's dad and his fiancée decided to sell both houses and find a new place. This suited Christine just fine: "I prefer living in a new house with this new family rather than having them move into my house."

In addition to deciding on living arrangements, you also will be faced with combining children with different interests and personalities. Just as you would do with your own children, recognize the individual strengths and talents of each child and validate them. Never compare a child who may be a poor student with one who is getting straight A's, or expect your uncoordinated son to play basketball with his star athlete stepbrother.

Christine now has a stepbrother her age. Although they are very different and have a separate set of friends, she proudly tells people he is a genius who has been offered a full scholarship to college. Remember, this boy reflects on his mother, who reflects on Christine's father. She likes the positive attention he brings to the whole family.

Tom is delighted to have stepbrothers. At first he was furious when his father told him he was getting married. "I said the *F*-word a lot," he says. "I didn't throw any real reason into my rant. 'You're not going to marry her!' They were going to do it in January, the middle of the school year. I asked them to wait, and they did. I was shocked, I guess. But then when I thought about it I was pretty all right with it. I'm lucky how it turned out. We ended up moving. I miss my old house a little, but this one is bigger. I have more people to hang out with. I like being able to go in the backyard and play football with my stepbrothers. It's definitely good. It could have been some random woman. I was kind of happy that I was going to get a couple of stepbrothers in there, too."

Nick blended his family when all the children still lived at home. "I don't think waiting would have made it any better. There's a lot of luck in the draw," he says. "I'm not sure there's a recipe that makes it work. We have six personalities in our house. You can't go to an AA meeting and find six people all alike. People are different from one another."

What saved Nick's situation is that his son and his new wife's son had been friends before their parents began dating, so even though both boys were against their parents' remarriage, they bonded through their allegiance to each other (and by making fun of the adults). If this happens to you, consider yourself very fortunate. Anything that tightens the bond between your kids and hers will strengthen the family as a whole.

In order to ensure that you combine your families successfully, Dr. Halpern recommends holding family meetings. And yes, your teenagers will almost definitely roll their eyes. But they'll come if you insist. "At these meetings, everyone has an equal say in terms of voicing their feelings and opinions. Nothing you say can be held against you. You can't be punished," he advises.

Dr. Halpern says that when you first come together to discuss the new rules of the house, make it a positive experience. "Tell them about built-in incentives and rewards, not just in terms of allowance and gifts, but privileges. If you're doing chores and becoming more responsible, you become entitled to new privileges."

A clear allocation of chores is important in a blended family. When it was just you and your kids you might have asked whichever child was nearby if he or she would walk the dog or take out the trash. And if one started to balk—"I always take out the trash. Ask Kathy!"—you weren't concerned that this would shake the foundation of your family. In a blended family, it actually can. It's not fair to any kid if he or she does household chores while a stepsibling is watching television. Not only will this disparity affect their relationship, it will also affect the one between you and your new wife. The injustice of your child doing all the work won't be lost on you, and it will work like a tiny crack that will keep growing unless something is done immediately to repair it.

Your family meetings—which should be weekly at first, then monthly once you've all settled into a routine—are the time and place to discuss the division of labor. Chores can include anything it takes to keep your household running, such as making dinner, walking the dog, mowing the lawn, folding and putting away the laundry, vacuuming, cleaning the bathroom, and taking out the trash.

You will be surprised how well all the children will get along, or at least tolerate one another, if you and your new wife parent as a couple and treat the children as "ours." Many kids, like Tom, actually become very close to their new siblings. Justin also likes that his mom's new husband has two kids younger than he is, because he gets to be a big brother.

Just as you had to help foster a respectful, loving, and noncompetitive relationship between your own kids, now you will do the same with your blended family in partnership with your new wife.

The Unexpected Bundle of Joy

Eighteen-year-old Jacki admired her reflection in the mirror as a seamstress pinned the hem of her prom gown. She was not prepared for what came next. "By the way," the seamstress said, "Congratulations! I can't believe your father is having a child!" Jacki was stunned. Her father had never mentioned that his new wife was pregnant.

When she later confronted her dad, he told her he had been waiting for just the right time to tell her that he and his wife were having a baby. But in the meantime, the entire neighborhood had already heard the news. This is no way for your kids to find out they are about to have a half brother or sister.

"I felt terrible because I didn't know," she says. "He

should have told my brother and me before they told all those other people. He could have taken us out for breakfast and told us the news. It would have been fine. But the way he handled it, he made it pretty clear that he had his new family, and we were on the outside."

Don't ever do this to any of your kids, regardless of which marriage or relationship they stem from. If you handle this honestly, once the initial shock wears off, your children may even be excited to learn they are about to have another sibling.

Communicate openly and reassure them that although the family is expanding, your relationship with them will not change. Include them in the process by keeping them informed of due dates and possible names. Buy a baseball glove and tell your son you'd love him to teach his new brother how to play, or let your daughter help decorate the nursery. Make sure they are involved in showers and parties before the baby is born as well as birth rites such as naming ceremonies and christenings. Even if this is difficult for your new wife, she will have to accept that your family includes all your children.

As a consequence of the way her father handled the situation, Jacki says she doesn't have a relationship with her six-year-old half sister. Even though they don't live far apart, her father rarely initiates joint outings and he arrives alone when he gets together with Jacki and her brother. "I see her twice a year," she says. "She loves my brother and me. But she's very confused about who we are, what our relationship is with her, and why we don't share the same mom. My dad has done nothing to foster our relationship with her."

This is a loss for everyone involved, and one that could have been prevented if Jacki's dad had considered all of his children to be part of one big, happy extended family rather than two sad, fractured units.

In many situations, the children from a first marriage are significantly older and may be too busy with school or work obligations to spend time with their half sibling. If this is true in your case, then don't insist that they do, but always continue to offer.

It Takes Discipline to Discipline

Recently, Nick told his stepson that he'd like to take the entire family back to Hershey Park, where they had vacationed years earlier. Nick says, "I told him I'd like to do it one more time while everybody is still at home. My son asked me, 'Why?' I said because the last time we were there it wasn't good. He asked what happened, and I said, 'You don't remember? You were being difficult and I took you by your arm and pulled you to the side of a building and chewed you out. It haunts me to this day. It was horrible. You don't remember that?' He said he didn't. I guess discipline is all in the perception."

As Nick learned, knowing when and how to discipline your stepchildren is complicated and potentially filled with a mass of emotions that can affect not only your relationship with that child but also your relationship with your spouse. You and your new wife must first be in agreement as to how to discipline the kids. When possible, discipline together as a unit, as the parents of all the children in the family. Obviously if there are minor issues such as a lack of manners, each stepparent has the right to remind the children of the basics of "please" and "thank you."

Since you are trying to strengthen the relationships in a blended household, you may be reluctant to be the bad cop with your stepkids. But this will change once you establish a trusting, respectful, and loving relationship with them. You may then find that you treat them like your own and, without thinking twice, discipline as needed.

Tracey was six when her father remarried and blended their two families. Because she was so young and genuinely liked her stepmom, Tracey says she was fine with the discipline being meted out by all three of her parents. "I didn't go through 'You're not my mom so you can't tell me what to do.'" Alan says both he and his wife discipline the younger children, who are hers from a prior marriage, because they live with them. "With my kids, [teenagers who remain with him half the time], my wife will call them on it and I'll take over the discipline."

Disciplining older children is difficult even in an intact family. Daniel, who acknowledges how nice his stepmom has been to him and does not want to do anything to undermine his father's marriage, says, "I just don't want to be torn between doing what I want and appeasing her. I'm not going to change my lifestyle. No way. Once you've been given freedom, who wants to go back to her rules? I wouldn't say anything to her, though. I'd say it to Dad."

Justin, who is very fond of his father's girlfriend, says if she ever yelled at him, he would feel angry and disrespected. "I wouldn't like her anymore if she yelled at me. I'd say, 'You have no right. You're not my parent.'"

So how do you handle a delicate situation such as this? You do your best to talk to your children as a couple, quietly and firmly. No yelling. A loud voice may work with your own child, who is able to move past it because he loves you unconditionally, but a stepchild's feelings for you are a bit more fragile even if you are close, and shouting can damage the relationship you are trying to develop.

Tom's dad and stepmom have apparently figured out how to discipline the children equally. When Tom was texting too much on his cell phone, resulting in an enormous bill, his dad and his stepmother talked to him together. He was ordered to pay them back or lose future birthday and Christmas presents and six months of allowance.

Handling discipline this way elevates your wife to a position of authority, which she should hold, and puts her on an equal plane with you, which is necessary for your marriage to survive.

The *Other* Dad

Not only is your child being disciplined by you and his stepmom, but if his own mother is remarried, he may very well be reprimanded by a stepfather. For most dads, this can be difficult to accept.

Drew says he becomes angry every time he learns that

his son has been punished by his ex-wife's husband, with whom he lives most of the time. Dr. Halpern understands this anger. "It's a painful ego thing. But discipline aside, if the stepfather is a good guy, then try to frame the relationship as positively as you can. Your son now has another strong male in his life, *and* the stepfather is not going to replace you."

While it may not be necessary for you to like your child's stepfather, you should always remain cordial because it's in the best interests of your children. "I tell parents who handle this poorly to get past their anger for the kids' sake," Dr. Halpern says. "In one couple I worked with, the two dads got into a fistfight at the son's bar mitzvah because they were unhappy with the seating arrangements. The police had to be called. People need to hear that this is damaging to your children. Keep your anger and rage to yourself."

Being polite and respectful to their stepdad will obviously make life much easier for your kids. If you can take it a step further and accept that your child can love this stepparent without losing any love for you, it will be healthy for both you and your child. "Use positive psychology—look at the benefits you have," he says. "There are two men who love your child and two guys with whom your kid can do things. It's not a competition."

Your children usually recognize how difficult it is for you when they develop a relationship with a stepdad. Justin likes his new stepdad, but he understands how important it is for him to remain close to his father, who's easily threatened by that relationship. "I do my best to get along with everyone," he says. Mike is also sensitive to his father's feelings about his having a stepdad one day. "He would get a little freaked out if I were hanging out with another father-figure type. I think that would really bother him."

You want your children to respect and bond with your new wife, and you can't expect them to do any less with their mother's new husband. Recognize the prickly situation in which your kids find themselves. They must maintain a genial relationship with their stepdad in order to maintain their relationship with their mother and peace at home. They might even like him. But at the same time, they don't want to be disloyal to you. If you can speak favorably (or at least neutrally) about their stepfather, you will lessen the burden on your children—a burden they never asked for in the first place.

If your relationship with a woman leads to marriage or cohabitation, your already struggling kids will face a whole new set of worries. Include them in family decisions, no matter how mundane, and give them back a sense of control over their lives. If you and your wife work as a true partnership and identify the special needs, talents, and concerns of all the children, you just might have a Brady Bunch after all.

Suggested Reading

1001 Ways to Be Romantic, Gregory J. P. Godek (SourcebooksCasablanca).

The Boomers' Guide to Online Dating, Judsen Culbreth (Rodale Press).

The Case for Marriage: Why Married People Are Happier, Healthier, and Better Off Financially, Linda J. Waite and Maggie Gallagher (Broadway).

The Complete Divorce Recovery Handbook, John P. Splinter (Zondervan).

The Complete Single Mother: Reassuring Answers to Your Most Challenging Concerns, Andrea Engber and Leah Klungness, Ph.D. (Adams Media Corp.).

Divorce and New Beginnings, Genevieve Clapp, Ph.D. (John Wiley & Sons, Inc.).

Good Husband, Great Marriage, Robert Mark Alter (Warner Books).

How It Feels When a Parent Dies, Jill Krementz (Alfred A. Knopf).

How to Go on Living When Someone You Love Dies, Therese A. Rando, Ph.D. (Bantam).

Mars and Venus on a Date, John Gray, Ph.D. (HarperCollins Publishers).

Men Are from Mars, Women Are from Venus, John Gray, Ph.D. (HarperCollins Publishers).

Reviving Ophelia: Saving the Selves of Adolescent Girls, Mary Pipher, Ph.D. (Riverhead Trade).

The Seven Levels of Intimacy, Matthew Kelly (Simon & Schuster).

The Shelter of Each Other: Rebuilding Our Families, Mary Pipher, Ph.D. (Ballantine Books).

The Single Parent Resource, Art Klein and Brook Noel (Sourcebooks, Inc.).

Stay in Lust Forever, Pamela Lister (Hearst Books).

Strong Fathers, Strong Daughters: 10 Secrets Every Father Should Know, Meg Meeker (Regnery Publishing, Inc.).

Surviving the Single Dad Syndrome, Kevin James (PublishAmerica).

The Ultimate Survival Guide for the Single Father, Thomas Hoerner (Harbinger Press).

The Wonder of Boys, Michael Gurian (Tarcher).

The Wonder of Girls: Understanding the Hidden Nature of Our Daughters, Michael Gurian (Atria Books).

Index

ELLIE SLOTT FISHER is the author of the critically acclaimed *Mom, There's a Man in the Kitchen and He's Wearing Your Robe*. A veteran journalist, Fisher's work has appeared in numerous magazines as well as in the anthology *Single Woman of a Certain Age*. A dating mom herself, she lives outside of Philadelphia, and has two children.

Visit elliefisher.com.

DR. PAUL HALPERN is a psychologist who counsels children, adolescents, and their families. He has maintained a practice in Villanova, Pennsylvania, for thirty years.